Pray Hard & Speak Life

Finding Hope in the Midst of:
Addictions
Bankruptcy
Suicide
Cancer

CLIFTON J. POWELL

WESTBOW
PRESS®
A DIVISION OF THOMAS NELSON
& ZONDERVAN

WestBow Press books may be ordered through booksellers or by contacting:

WestBow Press
A Division of Thomas Nelson & Zondervan
1663 Liberty Drive
Bloomington, IN 47403
www.westbowpress.com
1 (866) 928-1240

ISBN: 978-1-5127-0688-8 (sc)
ISBN: 978-1-5127-0689-5 (hc)
ISBN: 978-1-5127-0687-1 (e)

Library of Congress Control Number: 2015912594

Print information available on the last page.

WestBow Press rev. date: 08/13/2015

Contents

To Tamika – thank you for standing by my side during the good times and the bad times. You are strong in faith, a loving mother and a daily blessing. My love for you will never end.

Preface

ॐ

Popularity is something I have chased since the day I could walk. Mom can verify this if needed. She has stories that date back to me as a toddler and how I would walk the grocery store aisles extending my arm to shake a stranger's hand followed by, "My name is Cliff. What's yours?" She would tell you that I have always wanted people to know my name. When she asked what my goal was in college, I responded, "For all twenty thousand people to know my name before I graduate."

I wanted to be known for who I was, but at the age of thirty-two my life was radically transformed. I gained new perspective on life and began searching for what my purpose was while I'm here on this earth. I shifted from wanting to be known for who I was to what I have accomplished to advance God's kingdom. However, it is not you nor is it your neighbor from whom I seek applause, it's my Father in Heaven who I will one day stand before and give account for all my decisions in life and what I did in the name of Jesus during my short time on this earth. This book was written with that purpose in mind.

In the pages ahead, you will walk with me as I take you on the journey of my life. With the turn of each page, you will learn some of my most personal secrets as I have exposed all of my weaknesses. Those who know me may be shocked to learn some of the things they will read as no one truly knew how far I had fallen away from God and how I had allowed the temptations of this world to take me places and try things that could have ended my life. I share the fairy tale story about how two friends fell so deeply in love that they could not miss a moment together along with the battles that nearly tore them apart only to be become closer than ever as they walk through a life that is faced with one tragedy after another until they learn to Pray Hard & Speak Life.

Reflections

Spending six days confined in a small hospital room provides a lot of unrestricted time that can be used many ways. Some people will pass the time by watching TV, while others may read a book. Most of my time was spent looking out a window while reflecting on my life, the choices I had made, and the blessings I had overlooked along the way.

In June of 2014, my wife and I, both in our mid-thirties, were coming up on our fifteenth wedding anniversary. I desperately wanted to make this one special for her, as I had put her through a lot of pain throughout most of our marriage. Due to poor financial decisions, anniversaries of the past were nothing more than simple dinner dates at best. However, the hard work I had put into my job the previous year paid off in commissions, and I made plans to celebrate early. In December of 2013, I booked a prepaid vacation to Cancun, Mexico, and planned on surprising Tamika when we arrived at the airport.

Our flight was scheduled to leave for the four-night, all-inclusive vacation on June 30, 2014, and my anticipation was building since it was going to be the most relaxing trip of our marriage. However, life throws a curve ball sometimes; then again, sometimes it throws you more than one. In April 2014, I was let go from a job that I thought I would continue for the rest of my life. Debating on what to do about the trip, I decided it was best to tell Tamika about my anniversary surprise so we could discuss whether we should try to recoup some of the money, sell the vacation, or keep our plans.

After weighing out our options, we decided to continue on with our trip. As we were counting down the days, we never imagined something would keep us from our first week-long vacation without kids since 1999. However, there was a three-inch mass that stood in our way.

"This room is so small," Tamika said disappointedly as she was wheeled into the room.

"It's definitely not Cancun," I replied as I took in the place we would call home for the next six days. As I opened the door of the tall, slender closet that was just wide enough to fit a pair of shoes, I reminded myself that it was not the quality of the room, but the quality of care we needed to focus on. Looking for a new location for our luggage, I noticed the window to the right of the closet and directly in front of Tamika's bed offered a view of a brick building, while the window to the left offered a view overlooking the city. It was the window on the left where I began to reflect back to the day when our love began.

I imagined a life together full of love, peace, and happiness. However, I was young and ignorant to ways of the real world, especially when it came to marriage. Statistically, we had a fifty–fifty chance of our marriage ending in a divorce, but at the time, I didn't know it. Besides, I was confident and knew we were meant to be together forever.

⟫◆⟪

I remembered telling her one night as she was lying in my arms, "Tamika, when we marry, our life together will be full of love, peace, and happiness. Our children will have the best personalities. I can see us into our nineties sitting on a front-porch swing holding hands while thinking back on the story of our life."

It was romantic, and life seemed perfect. I thought our love was untouchable. However, I was young and ignorant to the ways of the real world, and as time passed by, I became complacent and unaware of the damage I was causing.

For the first ten years of our marriage, I battled addictions, selfishness, and pride. I put us through a lot of financial stress while Tamika battled putting up with a self-centered, chauvinistic jerk and tried her best to keep our marriage together. We both knew we were meant to be together until death did us part; however, the longer we stayed together, the worse our marriage became. Simple conversations that started with small talk would turn into what I call the "he said–she said" arguments. My frustration would build and build until I finally blew my top. Words of divorce were spoken many times during these arguments, but thankfully Tamika was full of faith and honored the covenant she made with God on the day we married.

———◆———

Turning from the window that overlooked the Nashville city skyline, I stared at my wife lying in the bed. I wanted to talk to her. I wanted to tell her how proud I was of her and how beautiful she looked, but she had fallen asleep and was resting peacefully. *It's best if I just let her rest,* I thought as I watched the movement of her chest while she slept. *I can't believe there's a tumor in there. Life is so precious and for so long, I took her for granted.*

I loved her more than I had shown her in the past fifteen years. I couldn't help but think back to the heartache I had caused from drinking and the stress I had caused from my poor financial decisions. They were all so clear to me now. *She should have left me long ago,* I thought. *I'm so thankful that she was such a godly woman who honored her vows; so many people don't. The words "to have and to hold, from this day forward, for better, for worse, for richer, for poorer, in sickness and in health, until death do us part" have such little meaning to so many people nowadays. I would have missed out on the best times of our marriage had she not taken her vows so seriously.*

As I walked over to her bed, I became full of joy and gratitude as I thought about God's grace; I thought about how He had rescued me from a path of destruction and placed me on a path that offered new life. It was His path that saved our marriage—a path full of light, which shined brightly and showed me the way as I traveled down this road we all call life. I wanted to let Him know that I recognized His mercy and grace and that I felt the urge to thank Him for the blessings He had given me. Speaking softly I said, "Thank You, Jesus."

Taking in her beauty, I stood next her, appreciating the breaths she was taking while tears ran down my face. I touched her head gently and thought about how much I wanted to swap places with her and be the one who was about to go through the pain and torture the next eighteen weeks would bring. Suddenly, I noticed how eerily silent the room was. Outside of the noise coming from her IV pump, there was not a sound. It was a silence that needed to be broken, as my thoughts were beginning to drift into a direction Tamika and I vowed we would not go. I knew it was time for me to reach out for help, and that help could only come for above. I laid my hand on her chest, and with a tone soft enough to not wake her, I began to pray over her life.

"Jesus, thank You for my wife You gave me. She is a perfect mate, and for so long I took Your gift for granted. I thank You for rescuing me from the Enemy and from myself. I'm now faithful and accept Your will, as it is the perfect will. But, God, if I have a say in Your will today, please heal my wife. If I don't have a say and Your will is to take her from me … then give me strength. Our life has had its share of tragedies; please don't let this be another. I need my wife. Our children need their mom. You're the Great Physician, and Your name is bigger than cancer. Heal my wife, Jesus. Amen."

As I completed my prayer, my head was still down, but my eyes lifted slowly and looked once again at the lady who helped transform me from the sinful man I was into a man filled with the love of Christ. I leaned over the arm of the bed and gently kissed her forehead while touching the beautiful, long blonde hair that would soon disappear. Feeling helpless, I turned back to the window, stared out into the skyline, and thought about the story of how our love came to be.

Balance

∞

Before we met, Tamika enjoyed painting, riding horses, and attending church, while I enjoyed the wilder lifestyle, pushing the boundaries and dreaded attending church. We were complete opposites, but we brought balance to one another. She has always been a spiritual person who believed the blood of Jesus could conquer anything. Truthfully, for the first ten years of our marriage, words like "blood of Christ" went in one ear and out the other. But after my life was transformed, I had a new understanding of what she spoke. Now that the Enemy had attacked her body, I pled the blood of Jesus over her daily.

I never understood God or how He worked until I was thirty-two. The preceding twenty years of my life were spent in a dark place enjoying the sins of the world. I developed a passion for drinking at the young age of twelve when I was fed drinks at an adult New Year's Eve party. Even though I became so sick that I swore I would never drink again, I found myself sneaking liquor from my dad's bar the very next week. This lifestyle carried over from junior high into high school where the passion extended from liquor and beer into dabbling with marijuana and LSD.

After spending most of my junior year in turmoil with my parents, I found a girl that stole my heart. My passion turned away from the poison of liquor, drugs and beer to the high school sweetheart who I felt for certain would one day carry my name.

The only good thing that came from that relationship was it kept me away from the temptations I once battled. The bad thing was, I trusted her with my heart.

I was sold out to her and committed my freshman year in college to our relationship. My Fridays and Sundays were spent on the road traveling so I could be with her. But in the spring of 1996, our relationship ended. I was hurt deeply and decided to turn back to the bottle. This began a journey with what I call "the Enemy" that took years to overcome.

It started out as having an occasional drink during the week; followed with drinking more heavily on weekends. In the summer of 1996, I began to hit the bars almost every night. The more I went out, the more connections I made. Connections that knew people and knew how to get certain things that were not found easily. My drinking eventually led to more drug abuse - the more I drank, the more drugs I tried.

I never planned on taking it as far as I did; however, holding back was never really in my plans either. If something new came along that I thought would make me feel like I had escaped this world, I would take it. Outside of heroin, meth and crack, there wasn't much that I had not tried. Was I an addict? At the time, I didn't think so. Looking back now, possibly I was. What is an addict anyway? Someone who has a difficult time saying no to temptations? If so, that was me. Someone who craved something? That was me. Someone who has a hard time quitting? That was not me - if I needed to quit for a while, I could. However, it might have been harder to quit had I not found what I had been missing my whole life at the age of thirty-two.

———◆———

When 1999 rolled around, I was a senior in college and was partying harder than ever before. I drank like a fish and was willing to take my drug abuse to the edge. I knew that I was playing Russian roulette and needed to change, but I wasn't ready. The fact is, I enjoyed dancing with the devil, and he loved leading our dance.

To earn money for the bills and my habits, I worked two jobs - as a bartender and as a waiter - both of which not only supported my habits financially but aggrandized them. The introduction of cocaine and ecstasy was made during my tenure as a bartender along with the introduction to new friends. Some of my friends in college were casual drinkers and steered clear of the harder side of partying while others walked the line of life and death.

Elliot was a shorter person in height but had a large personality. Standing around five feet three inches tall with a thin profile and black curly hair, he was one of those guys that girls thought to be adorable. Being one of the most likeable people I had ever met, I admired him for his kindness and ability to get along with anyone. No matter where we would go, I remember him being able to walk into a room and everyone seeming to know him. He never met a stranger without introducing himself and striking up a conversation and always seemed to find some type of common interest. I believe he did this in order to be able to relate to his new friends and make them feel at ease.

Though charming, genuine and very likeable he was also a heavy drinker and loved to smoke marijuana. One night Elliot came home from the bars drunk and most likely stoned. Hungry from the effects of his partying Elliot decided to cook a pizza. After starting the oven, he found his way to the couch to watch some TV.

The partying must have been pretty intense that night, because it did not take him long to fall asleep. The pizza cooked, and the timer probably went off, but the oven stayed on causing the pizza to burn. Without anyone there to turn off the oven, a flame ignited catching the pizza on fire. The flame inside the oven intensified as oxygen from outside the oven fueled the fire to the point of reaching the walls of the house ... Elliot did not budge. Passed out on the couch, Elliot never changed positions as the entire house burned to the ground. A person who brought so much joy to so many people in this world was lost that day due to a night that began with a single drink chosen of his own free will.

———◆———

Free will is a blessing given to us by God. If we choose to seek His advice on which path to take, life can be seen clearly, but choosing incorrectly can lead to devastation. The choices we make in life are nothing more than simple gates which lead to a path. Some gates lead to a safe path which contains a lot of light. The light comes from above and will guide you until you arrive at another decision or gate. But beware; if you choose incorrectly, the path on the other side of the gate will contain darkness, fear and depression.

This path is misleading as it may appear to be full of new adventure and excitement. New friends can be made along this path giving you a false security as you fall into the worldly trap of popularity. This path manipulates things to appear cool and adventurous while they couldn't be further from the truth. You may feel independent and free at first, but the longer you stay on this path, the more captured by darkness you become. The excitement turns dull, and you could find yourself seeking more danger to create excitement.

Life can be easy on this path as the Enemy has you where he wants you. On this path, you may find fame and riches but one day you will make a turn thinking it's the way out. You realize you are lost and begin to panic. You begin running and hiding trying to stay away from the temptations that surround you. But you can't hide when you're on this path. There are too many peers that know how to place pressure on you until you cave. You begin missing home. The safe innocent place of childhood is what you crave during the times you are sober. You being to cry out for help on the inside but no one can hear you. You don't think anyone is listening, and you begin to lose all hope.

Your independence is replaced by dependence, leaving you to rely on something that is not of God. The ones you considered friends are consumed with their own struggles and cannot be the friend you hoped for. Lives are broken, dreams are shattered, and loved ones are left alone praying for a miracle to save your soul. And God hears their prayers.

God is always with you, never leaving your side as He watches over you while instructing you on how to make the right choice. It's up to you to hear Him as His voice is a mere whisper. If you fail to listen, His heart aches as erroneous choices are made which widens the gap between you and Him. He longs to draw near to you but will not force Himself onto you as He knows free will is at stake. Like the father of the prodigal son in Luke 15, God will run to you when you seek Him but not until you seek Him.

It's the free will He is honoring that allows our independence to make our own choices. Dependence is a bondage that keeps you from being free. The Enemy uses bondage to keep you from God. However, if you call on Jesus, the bondage will be broken, and you will be rescued from the darkness as your past is forgiven and is replaced with new life. If you are bound and in a dark place, cry out for Jesus; tell him you are a sinner and need Him to forgive you. Tell Him you give Him your heart and beg Him to send the Holy Spirit to cleanse you. If you do, you will have a new start. But I warn you to choose your gates wisely. Seek wisdom from Him as He will guide you. If you don't and put your trust in yourself again, beware as you still have free will and the Enemy is there waiting on you to make the wrong choice. Turn from the Enemy by praying daily and walking with Christ where the light shines brightly and abundant life can be found.

I had chosen the wrong gate. Had I resisted the temptations before me, I would not have been traveling down a path full of darkness. I found myself lost, confused and lonely. I wanted to escape the path I was on, but the option of leaving seemed to decrease daily. The battles with addictions were pulling me into the darkest place I had ever been. A friend's life had been lost, my purity was replaced with dirtiness, and the dream of one day getting married was crushed years ago. I needed someone to come along that would shine some light into my world of darkness, but my heart was hard and I would not allow myself to get close enough to a girl to even begin to have feelings.

My parents didn't raise me to be the way I turned out. I was taught to work hard, respect others, respect elders and respect women. We attended a Baptist church, however I tried my best each Sunday to avoid going. I remember trying to come up with excuses as to why I couldn't go or didn't need to go. Sometimes, I would sleep as late as possible to run us late so we would have to miss. My antics never turned out good for me, but I was willing to take a belt versus go to church. A belt across my backside was pain that lasted minutes, church was pain that lasted for hours. However, there were days when I suffered both the pain of the belt followed by the pain of church. When we did attend, I rarely paid attention and didn't care to try. All I knew about Jesus was that He died for our sins and He loved His little children. Honestly, none of that made any sense to me at the time; besides, the last thing on my mind was Jesus. However, Jesus was on the mind of my future mother-in-law, who prayed for her daughter to marry the right man. If she had really known the state I was in, she would have prayed harder, thinking God made the wrong choice. But God is never wrong. Sometimes it just takes time to understand His purpose.

Adoration

oJlo

Because we had been married for fifteen years, you would think we would know the purpose of our marriage. But it was something I'd never given much thought or at least not until the mass in Tamika's chest was discovered. For those who have not been affected personally by cancer, it will put things into a new perspective. At first, our fear of the unknown took control. Then we decided to change our perspective and focus on defeating the Enemy no matter the cost. We prayed that our situation would lift others up and be meaningful while making a difference in the lives of others. The hardest prayer was one that we prayed often. We asked for the will of Jesus to be done, even if that meant the worst. It takes a lot of faith to pray that prayer: faith I didn't have nor understand throughout the majority of my life. Prior to our wedding day, I was a carefree, live by the seat of your pants, rebellious kid who had no ambition to grow up. However, all that changed due to one of my classes at the University of Alabama in January of 1999.

Child Psychology was required for my degree in Education. It was a large class, and I knew the professor had no way of truly knowing if you were there or not without sending around an attendance sheet. It was the perfect kind of class for me since the environment always allowed me to either sleep in late or catch up on the Andy Griffith reruns. Most classes of its size did not take attendance, and the professor just assumed if you did not attend you would not pass. This professor was different; he took attendance and if you missed more than three times, you failed. This left me in a predicament that I had to get out of, but I wasn't sure exactly how ... until I saw Kori.

Kori and I had a long history together that ran back to our early childhood. She and I grew up down the road from each other and throughout high school she was one of my closest friends. I felt like I could count on Kori to help me out and asked her if she would sign me in on the days I was absent. I explained to her how much I enjoyed watching Andy Griffith and the class was being offered during two back to back episodes. I'm not really sure why she did it, but Kori agreed, and I walked away with a system in place to make sure that if I failed it was not due to absences.

At least a month or two passed by before I saw that classroom again. So when I walked in, I surveyed all three sections trying to find my friend so I could sit by her. As I looked around I thought to myself, *no Kori, no Kori, no Kori. What! No Kori! She is supposed to let me know when she was not going to be here!!* Feeling frustrated, I went to the section Kori sat in the last time I was there. *Maybe she is just late.* I thought to myself as I turned around to see if there were any signs of Kori, but she never came. I was worried about the fact that she had failed me. I wondered if this had happened before. While I pondered over the situation I was in, I decided I needed a backup to Kori. I looked over at the girl sitting next to me and saw Kori's friend that lived next to her. Not knowing her name, I said, "Hey, has Kori ever missed class before?"

"No, this is her first time. She must be sick or something."

I felt a sense of relief flow through my body as we engaged in small talk. The topic of discussion was irrelevant to me as my mind was focused on one thing, getting her to become the backup to Kori. By the end of class, I learned her name was Tamika and she had agreed to sign me in if Kori and I were both absent. However, I was not convinced that I could trust my academic career on her tentative "*okay*" and began to realize that I must make sure she was capable of pulling it off. I needed to get to know her a little better so as class was dismissed, I chased her down the sidewalk. "Hey Tamika, wait up ... I'm having a few friends over for a pregame party before the game this Saturday. I thought you might want to bring some friends and check it out."

"I have a boyfriend."

"Cool, he can come too. Just pull into the parking lot and look for the crowd ... you'll find my place." I pointed out my apartment complex which was only a couple of blocks away as she began to continue her journey to her car. Honestly, I didn't think she had it in her to show that weekend, but when Saturday rolled around, Tamika was there.

Between Kori and Tamika, I knew that I was covered and didn't attend the class again for another two months. In place of class, my time was spent watching *The Andy Griffith Show* and the occasional movie every now and then: just not the kind on the big screen; they were too expensive for me. I had to wait for the VHS rental to come out and watch it. The days of renting movies at stores have now been replaced with vending rentals and digital media. In case you're not familiar with the process of a store rental, basically it's three easy steps:

>*Step 1- Rent the movie.*
>*Step 2 - Watch the movie.*
>*Step 3 - Return the movie.*

Steps one and two were never a problem for me; I could get myself to the store without any problems; I had no issues getting the card that would allow me to rent, and I had no problem at all watching the movie. But step three was a different story. I could not accomplish the third step to save my life.

The insanity began my sophomore year when overdue fees began adding up. Over time it got to the point that I was too embarrassed to go to the store. I would eventually owe more in late fees than what the store would sell the movie to me for. Once it came to this point, I would give in and purchase the movie to avoid being on the no rental list. This purchase would normally be made with what I called a t-shirt credit card. For those of you, who are unfamiliar with a t-shirt credit card, allow me to explain.

Throughout various parts of the campus were vendors that had tables set up containing Alabama t-shirts. They would ask if you wanted a free t-shirt. I was broke and in college, so when someone said free, I jumped.

"What do I have to do to get one?" I would ask while walking up to the table.

"All you have to do is complete this form and you get a t-shirt." the vendor would reply. I was ignorant to the bait they were using and would sign up each time. Over a period of two years, I brought home five t-shirt credit cards. Each one was used improperly, but I didn't care. I just blew it off and said I would worry about it later, thinking later would never come ... but it did.

Paying for the overdue movies with t-shirt credit cards worked great until my senior year. I ran out of credit, and my cards were all declined, leaving me with no option but to stiff that store and move on to the next. This crazy way of renting movies became the norm for me, and the next thing I knew, there was not a rental store in Tuscaloosa County that would rent to me. I enjoyed watching movies and had to come up with another plan, Kori ... I'll call Kori. "Hey Kori, this is Cliff. Do you mind renting a movie for me? I will pay for it, watch it and then you can take it back so I don't mess you up." I'm sure you can just imagine what kinds of questions I received. But Kori believed in me and being the kind hearted person she was, I was able to get back into the movie rental business!

The drive to Kori's apartment also took me to Tamika's. In fact, the only difference was when I parked at Kori's my car faced east; when I parked at Tamika's my car faced west. I was really close with Kori and always parked east. She and I became best friends that year and spent a lot of time together. I never mentioned it to her, but I grew very fond of her and began to have feelings for her that would have taken our friendship to another level had she felt the same. I never had the opportunity to find out. Fate stepped in our path and extinguished the romantic feelings I was beginning to have for my good friend forever. Ironically, she is the one responsible for the moment my life changed forever.

I probably called on Kori for a movie at least four or five times a month over the previous eight months. She had always been happy to help until a day in mid-January 1999. After being turned down, I hung up the phone, and I sat in disbelief. As silly as it sounds, I couldn't help but wonder how I was ever going to rent any movies. No one I knew would be so kind. Most of my friends would tell me where to go if I asked them. I needed someone with a loving heart, someone who could see the good in me even though I had darkness all around me. There was only one other person I could think of … Tamika. I lifted the phone and dialed her number. When she answered, I began my embarrassing story of how I could not rent from any store in town. After telling her the story of how irresponsible I was, she laughed and agreed to rent the movie.

"Really?" I was shocked.

"Yes, just come pick me up and I will ride with you."

I felt like a kid on Christmas morning. Grabbing my keys with a large smile on my face, I thought to myself, *my back-up saved me again!* I ran out the door, down the two flights of steps, hopped into the car and headed to Tamika's. When I arrived, I almost parked east out of habit, but I caught myself, backed up and parked west! Kori popped open her door with a cute little grin on her face and said, "What are you doing?"

I turned around with a big smile and said, "Do you see which way I am parked?"

Humbly she replied, "I do."

"From now on this is the way you will see it parked. I have found a new best friend, Kori. I'm sorry, but you have been replaced."

Kori laughed and said, "Whatever." She thought I was kidding and unaware of how my life was about to change, I also thought I was kidding.

I really didn't expect my trip with Tamika to the rental store to take more than thirty minutes. But, *Simon Birch* was a popular movie that had just been released at the stores, and Tamika asked if she could watch it too. I couldn't help but wonder why she wanted to watch the movie. *Maybe this is her way of keeping it in her possession to ensure it was returned.*

Tamika was not married nor was she engaged the day we rented the movie, however her life seemed only have one direction but that direction was about to change forever as the words we spoke that night were laced with innocent passion. As the conversation went on I could feel the vibrant energy drawing us closer together until we were within inches of touching lips. I was nervous. I had never felt a feeling so powerful before. My mind kept racing back to all the times I had promised myself that I would never fall for another girl. I was far from convinced that I was ready to trust anyone with my heart as it still ached from the results of a failed relationship from years ago ... until the moment we kissed.

Inseparable

✐

On the inside, I was nervous and concentrated on remaining calm. The girl I viewed as nothing more than a friend now had a different appearance. She was radiant; her gorgeous, blonde hair was soft between my fingers as they moved around the back of her head tenderly. The fullness of her lips perfectly matched with mine brought a whole new appreciation to the act of a kiss. I slowly moved my hands down her face and held them there taking in the new beauty I saw in her. A recollection of the pain from my last relationship ran through my mind, and I couldn't help but wonder if I was making a mistake … a mistake that could create more heartache. However, when the kiss ended, something on the inside told me this was different. There was something special in our kiss - something I had never felt before - I discerned that we were meant to be together, forever. By the time our night ended, I was confident that I had found the girl I would spend the rest of my life with.

Tamika and I became inseparable. Unless one of us had a class, we were together. I found myself searching for reasons to be with her and she found herself doing the same. We would often go out for a snack as early as 9:00 a.m. just to have an excuse to be together. The snack would usually lead to one of us riding with the other to run errands or go to the store, which always led to spending the day together. It was perfect and I was counting on it staying that way, but she had something that weighed on her heart as well as her mind. She knew there was a relationship that had to be undone.

My apartment consisted of three rooms. As you opened the door you entered the main area which was large enough to fit the small couch, one end table and a small coffee table. Towards the back of the room was a small kitchen which had a counter top separating it from the living room. At the end of the couch was an opening that led to my bedroom. Looking right you would see single box spring on the floor with a mattress directly on top. Up the wall, above my pillow was a window with an ac unit that hung directly above where I laid my head each night. To the left was my closet, again no door, and next to it was the restroom. As you turned around and to walk back into the living room was a skinny entertainment system and my television sat on top. To the left of it was the only empty area in my apartment. It was there that I was dancing slowly with Tamika when she made a decision that earned my respect forever.

"Cliff, I need to leave town and try to sort through some feelings." Her head was resting on my shoulder as we slowly swayed in tune of the music.

"I know you do." I replied as I gently pulled her a little closer to me.

"I'm just so confused by all of this. I'm afraid that my feelings will return when he comes back in four months. That wouldn't be fair to you and I don't want to mislead you. I never imagined someone different in my life and I must sort through these feelings."

"Tamika, I understand and I want you to go. You need to know for sure before we carry this any further. The last thing I want is for you to make a mistake and realize it after it's too late. If you come back and need to end what we have - I will still respect you. But I'm not worried because what we have is special and I know in my heart that you will choose me."

I knew what Tamika and I had was not a normal relationship - it had purpose, and I was confident that she would be mine forever. However, I wanted no regrets and our future together deserved a clear conscience from both parties. In life, it is important to do the hard things that must be done. If you choose to avoid what is difficult, you only open up the door for the Enemy. It was not easy, but setting Tamika free was something I knew had to be done. She needed to gain perspective on her feelings toward me. If she did not go, the confusion would only drive a wedge between us so I picked up the phone and helped her book a flight that possibly could have taken her away from me forever.

"Do you need a ride to the airport?" I asked as I walked her to her car.

"As much as I want you to go with me, I think I need to make this trip on my own." Her hands felt warm as she placed them in mine and I noticed how beautiful her brown eyes looked as they stared into mine. "Are you going to be ok while I'm gone?"

"I'll be fine. You need to get closure and if you don't find it during this trip I will wait because I know in the end you will choose me. Tamika, there's something I haven't told you yet. It's kind of silly but I want to share it with you. The night we kissed - I pictured our children coming to me and asking how I knew you were the one for me. Do you know what my answer to them was?" As she shook her head no I said, "The moment we kissed."

Time moved slowly over the next 72 hours. No matter how hard I tried, I could not stop thinking about Tamika. This was the longest we had been separated since the night of our kiss, and time was creeping by at a torturing pace. I tried to keep my mind off of her by staying busy, but nothing seemed to help.

When Sunday finally rolled around, I was hoping to sleep through the day long enough for her plane to land, but the nerves inside of me woke me up earlier than normal. I had a full day of waiting and needed something to keep my mind off her decision. But nothing I did could pull my mind away from pondering over what she had learned about her feelings. Deep down, I knew that she would choose me, but what I didn't know was how long I would have to wait.

When the time came for her flight to land, I sat on the couch and watched the phone as if I would be able to see it ring. Anticipation began to increase more and more with every passing minute. I tried to watch a game on TV, but it was not nearly as entertaining as watching the phone sitting on the end table just waiting for its opportunity to ring. *Ring, phone, ring ... please!*

Seconds turned into minutes and the minutes turned into hours. I thought to myself, *she must be at home unpacking and will call when she is done.* But as another hour passed, worry began to set in. *Why hasn't she called? Surely she will.* Unable to hold back any more, I lifted the phone and extended my finger to dial the number but quickly put it back down. I couldn't make myself call as I knew it was best to give her the space I promised. When the second hour passed, I began to get the lump in my throat that always appears when I face a major disappointment. *Could I have been wrong? Did I really help the girl of dreams book a flight to a destination that carried her away from me forever?* As doubt began to take the place of my confidence, I began to slump into a dark, sad place - the kind of place where a person is only able to get out by the help of doctors and medicine or God or ... ... the ringing of a phone! I jumped up like Jesse Owens and grabbed the phone "Hello!"

"Hi Cliff."

"Tamika! How are you?"

"I MET STEVEN TYLER!"

"What?"

"I met Steven Tyler and Joe Perry at the airport, and I rode on the same plane with them! I got their autographs and Steven Tyler even asked me to sit by him!"

"No way! Did you sit by him?"

"No, I mean, I would have, but I thought that maybe his bodyguard didn't want me to. It's a long story; I will just have to tell you when I get there."

"Okay," I said.

"Will you be up?"

"Definitely; just come on by." I hung up the phone and joy came across my body. It was a feeling that no drug had ever given me. The doubt had left my body and had been replaced by confidence. I knew for sure now that she had chosen me, but I was wrong.

When Tamika arrived, she embraced me with a hug and said, "You are not going to believe what happened to me today." I was trying to pay attention but was so overwhelmed by my happiness that I could barely focus on her words as she dove into her story. "As I approached the boarding gate, I could not believe who I was boarding the same plane. Cliff, not ten feet away from us, stood Steven Tyler and Joe Perry! Look, I have Steven Tyler's autograph and everything."

At first, I assumed that she had ended the relationship but the more she told her story, the more I realized it was not so. "My original flight was canceled and I was led to another terminal. It was a secluded area away from the normal gates and here I am all torn up because I have to leave. I mean I was a wreck emotionally and was crying when Steven Tyler asked if I was okay. It was difficult but I gathered my composure to tell him I would be fine and they boarded the plane."

"Tamika, that's amazing."

"Wait, that's not all. As I stepped inside the plane, Steven Tyler offered me the seat next to him."

"No way. Did you sit by him?"

"No! I was still very upset and nervous. I was unsure what to say. I took a step into the aisle by then a big man stood up. I figured it was his bodyguard trying to prevent me from getting to the seat."

"Wait, you don't think he was getting up to let you in."

"Maybe, he was. Anyway, I told him that I would just sit in my seat which was only two rows behind them. Can you believe that?"

I was hoping that Tamika found all the answers while she was away. Instead, she returned still in limbo and needed more time. That left me with one of two choices: be confident or be defeated. This was easy for me; I knew that we were meant to be together, and I was as calm and cool as James Dean.

As we sat on the couch, Tamika reached over and grabbed me hands before speaking her next thought. "I'm sorry Cliff. I know you were hoping that I would come back knowing who I needed to be with. But honestly, this weekend really confused me more than ever. I care a lot about you and don't want to hurt your feelings at all, but when I was away, I realized that I do still have feelings that need to be dealt with. I'm so sorry. I know this is hard."

"Tamika, don't feel like you have to apologize. I know in my heart that you will be with me and I will give you as much time as you need. I want you to be absolutely sure that you have made the right choice when you decide."

I tried my best to not put any pressure on Tamika at all. She had a hard enough decision to make without me pulling her my way. The night we found ourselves together in a kiss, I was not searching for love, but love was searching for me. I knew in my heart she would be mine so I gave her all the time she needed and we tried to meet as just friends. However, there was no denying that we were both deeply in love with one another.

Delicacy

It was during our first trip to Walmart together that I learned the ritual that takes place when you purchase a carton of eggs:

- *First, check expiration date.*
- *If it is good, then you proceed to open the container and look for damaged goods.*
- *If you find a damaged egg, then check your surroundings for witnesses of the act you are about to commit.*
- *Once you know no one is looking, you swap the damaged eggs with good eggs from another carton and quickly close the lid.*
- *Finally, gently you place them safely into your buggy, and walk away as if you are not guilty at all.*

This taught me how fragile eggs really are. They must be handled with care. It's the shell that contains the most important part of the egg. If the shell was not there, the delicacy would not be held leaving the egg in a mess instead of being held safely as it was meant to be.

We enjoyed grocery time together no matter where we went, but Walmart was a place we could people watch and cruise down the aisles holding hands looking at this and looking at that. To me, Walmart was more like an educational field trip. I would use this time to learn more about the one that I knew would be sitting by my side on a front porch swing up into our nineties.

She would always point out things that she liked or one day she hoped to have. She would point out things like lamps, pictures and frames. One day, we were strolling through the bedding section and there was this one item in particular that was more important than all others. I took mental notes of that piece and tried to make the best of it when the time was right.

I knew Valentine's Day could be a turning point in our relationship and decided to try a risky approach. On the eve of a day historically marked by marriages, romance and love stories, I chose to start an argument. I needed a reason that could spill over into the next day in order to capture the heart I was after. It was not easy, but sometimes in life the hardest things you do prove to be the most rewarding.

Tamika was already discouraged because she had to work on Valentine's Day, and I knew when I picked up the phone I was about to create a pain that she could not understand. "Tamika I want to get my CD's as well as anything else you have of mine out of your apartment. Can I come by and pick up a key while you're at work?"

"Why? I just don't understand, Cliff. Two days ago, we were fine and now I feel like your cutting me out of your life forever. I just don't get it."

"Can I just come by and get the key?"

"Sure. I guess."

"Thank you, I will be there in a few minutes."

As I walked into the office I barely looked at her. It broke my heart having to put her through what I was doing, but I knew it had to be done.

"Why are you doing this?"

Ignoring the question again, I grabbed the key she had laid out for me on the countertop and said, "Thanks, I will return it when I'm done," then walked out the door. I knew I was flirting with losing her with the actions and attitude I was displaying, but I didn't care. I was all in on this one. I knew it crushed her heart as she had never seen this side of me before but I remained focused.

Later that evening, Tamika came home to a box of goodies delivered by the UPS driver and she reached out to thank the giver via a phone call. During the middle of the conversation she noticed there was a hump in her bed. *What is this,* she thought to herself. Losing focus on the conversation taking place over the phone, she began to run her hand across the mattress confused by the texture she felt. Her curiosity was rising and she had to see what was under her covers. Slowly she pulled back the comforter, moved the pillow and lifted the fitted sheet. Stunned by what she saw she said, "I gotta go ..."

"What?"

"I gotta go ... I'm sorry!"

Without even saying goodbye, she hung up the phone. After finding her keys and running out the door, she jumped into her car and sped to my apartment in disbelief. When she walked in, I knew that my efforts had paid off. I apologized for the argument that I had staged and held her tightly. As I mentioned earlier, eggshells hold the delicacy that we desire, and the new eggshell mattress on her bed would be holding mine.

Game Changer

♪♪

Shortly after the eggshell was discovered, Tamika knew she had to end what was started so many years ago to begin the new chapter in her life. The effort from the other end to hold on was powerful. "This is so hard Cliff. I know it is hard on you too. I want to be with you, but I feel obligated to go one last time."

"Tamika, there is not a doubt in my mind that you will be with me, but I need you to be with me one hundred percent. If you feel that you need to go in order to make sure you are making the right decision, then that is what I want you to do. Please, trust me when I tell you that I'm okay. I do not want you spending the rest of your life with me while questioning yourself on whether you made the right decision or not." I didn't want her to leave, but I knew it was for her to have no doubts or regrets so for a second time, I had to trust the woman I loved would return to me.

Just like before, time moved at such a torturing pace-I might as well have been watching a snail race a turtle in the fifty yard dash. No matter what I did, I could not get her off my mind. When the time came for Tamika to return, I was overcome with relief. I was relieved that she had gone. I was relieved that she was back. I was relieved to know that she would be mine forever.

Now that she could move forward with her life, Tamika and I continued to spend every minute we had together. The time we spent enhanced our relationship. We loved one another dearly and knew that we would one day marry. However, we never imagined just how soon that day would come. It was now June and Tamika was lying next to me on the couch telling me about the wedding she had attended over the weekend.

I was stroking my hands through her soft blonde hair while her head rested on my lap when Tamika softly spoke up saying, "I was not able to fit into my dress."

"What do you mean?"

"I mean, the top was too small."

"So they made it a little too small."

"No, Cliff. I tried it on just three weeks before the wedding while at home. It should have fit fine." Tamika had now raised her head off my lap and grabbed my hands. Looking into my eyes the words she spoke next caught me by surprise. "Cliff ... I think I may be pregnant."

I stood up and began to pace around the room taking in what she had just said. "Pregnant ... really?"

"I really think I am. The top not fitting is not the only sign, Cliff. I missed my last cycle and I have been feeling a little sick lately."

Looking down at the beige carpet on the floor, I began to rub above my eyes as I began to picture our life. After a long pause of silence, I reengaged in the conversation. "I guess we need to go and get a test. Do you want to get one from a store or wait and see the doctor?"

Tamika must have sensed my anxiousness as she grabbed my hand when I walked by. She gently pulled me back to the couch and rubbed my leg as if saying, calm down. Softly she leaned her head on my shoulder and almost in a whisper said, "I prefer we get one to take at home, and then we will see if we need to go to the doctor or not."

Her efforts to calm me down worked a little, but I was still anxious.

Trying to break up the tension I replied, "Why don't we go ahead and get two in case the first one lies?"

Tamika laughed and agreed with my idea. We both stood up and grabbed our things to head out the door. The closest pharmacy was within a mile distance so it did not take long for us to pick up two of the top brand pregnancy tests and head back to her apartment. She was nervous and had me look at the results for her.

"Does the minus sign mean negative?" I said kiddingly as an effort to break the tension.

"Yes … Cliff … the minus means negative."

"Then you are pregnant according to this one. Don't panic though. Next time you need to use the restroom take the other one and let's see what it says. These things are only 98% accurate." This came with a smile on my face. I wanted her to know that no matter the outcome, I would be with her.

During the next hour, the nervousness Tamika and I felt were overshadowed by feelings of joy and excitement. My anxiety had calmed, and the reality of us being together forever began to sink in. We began discussing our concerns about spending the rest of our life together as a family. We talked about how we should tell our friends and family. Tamika and I were genuinely in love with one another and truly were okay if she was pregnant. Sure we were aware of the challenges we would face, but as the time passed, we enjoyed discussing our future and overcoming the challenges together.

By the time Tamika was ready for the second test, we were much more comfortable with the results, which came back positive. Tamika scheduled an appointment with her gynecologist and three days later it was confirmed that I was going to be a father.

I thought a lot about my future and how I could not continue the road I was on. I had told myself that if the doctor confirmed her pregnancy I would stop all partying and completely change my ways. I had been drinking for eleven years and tinkering with other stuff for more than seven. I knew this was a game changer and nothing would ever be the same. I had to change my ways and decided the best way to achieve my goal was to isolate myself by staying as busy as possible. I called my closest friends to inform them that I would no longer be going out on the town and living the lifestyle of the past. I was to be a husband and a father soon and needed to begin a new life.

Tamika and I knew this was going to be difficult on our families and decided the best approach was to be confident and specific with our future. We discussed our options and came up with a plan that would help ease the tension when we presented the news to our parents. There was no doubt in our minds that we wanted to spend the rest of our lives together; it was now just a matter of when and how we would marry. Multiple options were discussed until we decided that early to mid-August would be best. It was a few weeks before fall semester started, and my sister's wedding was in July, which would allow a small window for planning in between.

Within the week, I had made plans to move home for the summer to take advantage of the local community college which offered classes that I needed to help me graduate in the coming December. I was also able to line up a temporary job at a local manufacturing plant. Tamika was my main concern, though, and I was very hesitant to leave her behind. However, my options were limited, and I was determined to do whatever was needed to start off my marriage and family the best way possible.

When I left my house for college, at the age of eighteen, I never imagined I would move back in four years later. I guess my parents thought the same, as they were surprised to learn that after coming home only during the holidays for the past three years, I would now be spending the entire summer with them. I guess in the back of my mom's mind, she knew that something was up, although she never led on until the day I had to break the news to her.

At age 20, Tamika was pregnant and all by herself as a sophomore in a strange town called Tuscaloosa. Though she was surrounded by 25,000 students, she felt isolated and alone, and things only got worse when she was admitted in the hospital for several days due to kidney stones. I desperately wanted to be there for her. However, classes and work had already started, so one of my closest friends at the time watched over her and kept me informed daily on how she was progressing until she felt well enough to go home.

The day after she was released from the hospital, Tamika and I discussed her moving to Cullman; she agreed it would be best. Truthfully, neither of us could take being separated from one another. For the past five months, we spent nearly every waking moment with one another and heartache would set in while we were apart. The decision was made, and the following day, she packed her bags for the summer and prepared to move in with a family she barely knew.

My sister's wedding was a month away the day Tamika left Tuscaloosa for Cullman, and my mom was already under a lot of stress, making it all the more difficult when it came time to confront her with my news. But sometimes hard things must be done, and it is much better to not procrastinate when it comes to the uncomfortable/difficult things in life.

Sitting at the kitchen table that overlooked the yard, which offered a beautiful view of the lake, I began to gaze out the window while mom was telling me about the upcoming wedding for my sister. We discussed my role in her wedding that would be held at a church, and I decided there would not be a more appropriate time to ease into my news.

"Mom, did you know the last time Tamika was here she mentioned having her wedding in our yard, even if we did not marry?"

Mom just laughed and said, "That would be a little awkward, but I guess it would be okay."

"Well, mom, her marrying someone else will not be the awkward part. The awkwardness will be the fact that she will be three months pregnant when we marry."

With a look of frustration, mom stared at me with big eyes and said, "That's great, Cliff! What are you going to do next to make my hair turn more grey?"

"I'm sorry mom, but we are really in love with one another. There is no doubt in my mind that she is the one I'm supposed to be with for the rest of my life. But I need you and dad to be okay with this. We are planning on getting married in August and Tamika has always wanted a simple outdoor wedding. This is the perfect spot, and I will do everything I can to take the pressure off of ya'll. All I ask is that you and dad be understanding and supportive. You have always wished I would settle down and quit partying, and I have now. I'm more focused on graduating than I have ever been, and I know my role as a husband, father and provider. It may be rough, but we are both determined to make this work. Tamika has been battling kidney stones along with morning sickness. She was in the hospital last week and needs to be here where I can help her. I hope it's okay, I told her to come here, and she could stay with us for the summer. She should be here this afternoon."

There was a long silence that filled the room as she contemplated on my proposal. Finally, I heard the words I had hoped to hear.

"Yes … it will be okay. I hope this settles you down. I've had about all I can take!"

"I understand mom. It has already settled me down. I'm aware of the responsibilities that lie ahead and will do everything I can to make it all work. Thank you for understanding."

After Tamika moved in, she battled morning sickness that seemed to last throughout each day during the first trimester of her pregnancy. While Tamika was trying to keep things down, I was trying to manage taking a class for two hours each morning followed by twelve to sixteen hours of work each day. It was hard on us both, but not as hard as the trip we took to Florence to tell her parents about our news.

———⦅⦆———

The drive seemed to take forever, and with each passing mile, I could feel the knot in my throat getting larger. I had only met her parents twice prior to this trip. The first time was very brief at her Uncle Albert's funeral; the second time was in Tuscaloosa. I really had no idea what kind of people her mom and dad were and was not sure if I was going to make it out of their house alive once they learned the news. I was more nervous than I had ever been in my life, and when we arrived, I felt nauseous, and my legs were shaking as if I had just completed a marathon. Taking in a deep breath to try and calm myself enough to gain control of my legs, I climbed out of the car and walked to the door that led to a conversation I was not looking forward to.

Tamika seemed more at peace with the situation as she was telling me her childhood memories. "Momma has always kept it pretty. She has added a lot of antiques since I was home last. Did I tell you they own an antique furniture store?"

"I don't think so."

"We can drive by it on the way out of town, and I will show it to you."

"That would be great, Tamika." Right about the time I finished Tamika's name her mom walked into the room.

Being that this was my first trip to her house and the third time to meet her mom. I anticipated anger and bitterness, but Tamika told me that her parents were not that way. Regardless, I had my doubts.

"Well ... This is a surprise! I wasn't expecting you home today," her mom said as she hugged her baby girl.

"Momma, you remember Cliff, right?"

"Why sure. You rode up with Tamika for Uncle Albert's funeral."

"Yes ma'am, I did," I spoke with confidence trying to mask my nervousness.

"That sure was very kind of you."

"It was my pleasure," again with confidence.

"I'm glad to see you, Tamika. But I was not expecting you, and you usually call me to let me know you are on your way. What brings you here without calling first?"

Tears began to run down Tamika's face as she struggled to find the words and as I looked up I could see sadness come upon her mom's face. "What's the matter Tamika?"

"Momma … I'm pregnant."

"Oh my, Tamika …" Silence filled the air for a few minutes as her mom reached for some tissue. By the time she handed Tamika some, they were both in tears and I was not sure if I was going to make it out of the room without crying myself. With this being my third time to meet her mom, I decided I would let Tamika do the talking unless I was asked a question directly. So, I just sat there and tried to keep it together and appear humbly confident.

"What are you going to do?"

"Mom, I have never experienced anything like what I feel for Cliff, and I know in my heart that we would marry one day. This is just going to make that day come a little quicker than we anticipated. But we love each other deeply, and we will be fine. Cliff only has one semester left before he graduates. I will attend classes this fall and finish up my degree after the baby is born."

Tamika's mom sat in silence and gathered her thoughts before speaking. "Well, Tamika, it sounds like you have a plan."

"We do, Momma. Should I tell Daddy?" Tamika asked with a tone in her voice that wished for an answer of no.

"No, baby, I will tell him. It will be better that way."

"I'm sorry I disappointed you, mom."

"Oh, Tamika, you have never disappointed me. Life throws us curves sometimes, and we just have to work our way through them and trust in the Lord that He will see us through. Besides, it sounds like you are now doing the right thing. I'm proud of you for that. You two seem to be happy together, and I'm confident that you will be fine."

"Thank you, momma, I love you so much. Tell Daddy that I love him too. We better go before he comes inside."

She was right. Her mom was loving and kind but most importantly receptive. She welcomed me into their family without judgment and made me feel loved from the start. They supported us and did everything they could to help us stay on our feet.

I guess it was about one week before our wedding when I officially asked Tamika to marry me. I was not sure if it was appropriate or not since we already had plans set and invitations sent out. But I wanted her to have the normal proposal experience and was willing to do whatever it took.

Since I was in college, broke and trying to save money for a baby, purchasing a nice diamond ring that she deserved was quite a challenge. I knew I had to come up with a way to get some extra money and thought about the rifle I used to hunt deer. It had a pretty nice setup and could probably bring enough to get a decent ring. The wedding was now less than two weeks away, so I really did not have time to run an ad in the paper. Instead I decided to take them to a pawn shop, which provided enough money for me to purchase a pear shaped diamond ring just like Tamika had always wanted.

Later in the day, as the sun was setting, I took Tamika for a walk around the back yard. As we walked in the area that we were to be married, we discussed the setup for our wedding. We talked about chair placement, how we could make sure the ducks participated, where we would stand and all other logistics. Tamika thought we had it all covered until I mentioned she was missing one thing. She questioned my comment as we walked down to the edge of the lake. I played it off as if I had not heard her questions and kept leading her to the prettiest location where I hit my knee, grabbed her hand and stared up into her beautiful brown eyes and proposed.

"Tamika, you mean more to me than anything in this world. From the minute we kissed, I knew that you and I would be together forever. Although our wedding date is set, I wanted you to have a traditional proposal. It would be an honor to go through life with you. Will you marry me?"

I pulled out the ring and slid it onto her finger. With tears running down her face she said, "Yes."

August 14, 1999

♪♫

Tamika was right; the yard was a perfect setting for a wedding. There was a large open area with just the right amount of pine trees to provide shade yet offered enough sunlight for a well-manicured lawn with ample space to host a small wedding. A hundred yard walk from the back door steps would take you to the best view in the lakeside subdivision. The view overlooked the public boat launch and the largest body of water the lake had to offer. The place was gorgeous and Tamika immediately knew how her wedding would look.

What she didn't know is that it would be considered one of the prettiest weddings most of the guests had attended. Friends and family pitched in to bring her dream to life. As she walked from the porch steps, she saw two sections of white chairs with an aisle in between. Ferns were placed at the end of each row of chairs. White pipes linked together with draped tulle carved the path that anticipated my fiancée. Two of the groomsmen unrolled white fabric to make her aisle. Halfway to the lake, an iron arbor was placed and dressed in tulle mixed with bouquets of yellow flowers completing the picturesque setting.

As the guests entered, they would hear beautiful melodies being played by the most talented violinist anyone in the crowd had ever heard. Everything would be peaceful in her mind. But the peace the wedding would bring did not come without a storm.

For me, the week leading up to our wedding was hectic. It started with a birthday dinner for my fiancée followed by school final exams for the summer semester, then wrapped up with the completion of my part time job I took over the summer. This was all on top of the gardening, lawn care, and painting that needed to be done around the house to prepare for a wedding. But nothing was more important to me than feeding the ducks.

At the time around our wedding date, ten ducks and one ugly turkey/duck looking thing meandered along the shores of the lake. Tamika has always been an animal lover and would feed them every day. Her favorite was the poor ugly duckling. I wanted to train them to swim over to our shore and walk in the background of the spot we would be reciting our vows. I told Tamika that I needed her to start feeding them each day in the exact same spot at 6:20 p.m. followed by an explanation as to why. If this worked, it would be one of the key elements to our outdoor wedding.

The events of the week made it pass quickly, and Friday was here before I knew it. Our day for dress rehearsal had finally come, but so did the threat of a storm. The storm was forecasted to hit our location after 6:30 p.m., so we decided to change our start time from 6:00 p.m. to 5:00 p.m. Thankfully, everyone was able to accommodate their schedules, and we stayed on track to end before the storm. It was a windy and wet storm that night but ended rather quickly and was over by the time we finished our rehearsal dinner around 8:00 p.m.

The storms that come on suddenly can be the scariest just like the storms of life. Tamika and I found ourselves caught in a storm that came on as sudden as an earthquake. However, blessings can also be found in the storm. One of our many blessings from the storm was a twenty degree drop in temperature.

In Alabama, mid-August usually reaches upper nineties to above one hundred degrees. Tie that in with a high humidity factor and your body would naturally sweat the instant you went outside in shorts and t-shirt, so we had concerns about the comfort of the wedding party and guests. Now that the storm had passed, we could rest assured that our wedding day would bring a mild seventy-five degrees and very little humidity.

During the night, someone decided to drape toilet paper rolls from our trees. I have to admit, they did a bang up job, and any other day I would have thought it was quite pretty. Nonetheless, it was 7:00 a.m. on our wedding day, the rain from the previous night's storms had left us a long list of tasks that needed to be completed prior to the arrival of our guests at 4 p.m., so I was not happy to see the list grow due to pranksters. Thank God for the family members and good friends that graciously pitched in; otherwise, we would not have pulled it off.

We mailed out one hundred invitations and felt we would be lucky if half attended. Tamika had feared the hour and a half drive from Florence would be too much on her friends, and most would not attend. She has always been loved by everyone, and it did not surprise me at all when she had more on her side than I had on mine.

Standing with my dad by my side, I mentioned to him how I was amazed to see the number of people attending. All sixty chairs were taken and we had another thirty or forty guests standing in the back watching from a distance. Unbeknownst to us, there was a fishing tournament kicking off at the moment of our wedding. As the bridesmaids were led by groomsmen, the sound of motor boats overtook the melody being played on the violin. Since the lake is small, it wasn't but a minute or two before the noise of the boats was gone.

One of the highlights came from two men fishing in the tournament. I don't know if they were watching our wedding or if the fishermen just off the shore really thought it was a hot spot to fish. Regardless, they stood with hats off as the tune of "Here Comes the Bride" played over the violin.

Tamika's beauty overcame me as she walked down the aisle. I couldn't hold it back and had to tell someone. "Isn't she beautiful,"

I whispered to Tamika's childhood pastor who was officiating our wedding. He grinned and gave me a wink of agreement. As Tamika completed her walk, a few whistles were heard in the distance. Looking back towards the lake, I saw the fisherman clapping and whistling as our wedding began.

"Who gives the bride away?" the pastor asked as he looked out into the crowd.

"Her mother and I," came from a voice filled with uncertainty and doubt.

I looked over at her father who appeared to have a tear in his eye and knew he was having a hard time letting go of his baby girl. I wish I could have eased his mind on that day, but outside of a promise to him that I would take care of her, there was nothing more I could do. At the time the vows were said, the ducks swam up to the shore and waddled up right behind the preacher for their evening meal. Everything was working out just as planned.

After the rings were exchanged, it was time to light the unity candles. The unity candles are made up of three candles with the tallest in the middle. The parents of the groom light the one on the right, and the parents of the bride light the one on the left. After the bride's parents are seated, the bride takes her parents' lit candle, and the groom takes his parents' lit candle; then, in unity, they light the middle candle and blow out the flames of their parents' candles symbolizing two becoming one.

Months later, Tamika's sister was watching our wedding video and noticed how the flame of our candle was blown out by the wind several times, but always relit. Personally, I believe the Enemy was trying to blow out our flame, but our God is bigger, and He kept our flame alive. To this very day, the Enemy is still trying to disrupt our marriage. But Jesus is the rock we stand on, and as long as we keep Him the centerpiece of our marriage, our flame will burn.

Holes

ℐℓ

It was 7:30 p.m., and I had just finished changing out of my tuxedo into the clothes I would wear to begin our honeymoon. A lifelong friend, Brannon, along with some other friends gathered around the bar in the basement of my parent's house when I walked in with disbelief. "Man, it's hard to believe that I'm married. You know just eight months ago, I had been at a Malcolm's wedding still vowing to never date again."

Brannon grinned and with a chuckle added, "That's right, Cliff. I forgot about that. Didn't this all begin with a garter belt?"

Anticipating a funny story, Tom smiled followed with, "A garter belt, I don't think I've heard this one."

I found my way to the middle of the bar and began my story. "It's funny how things happen. I never would have imagined in a million years when I picked up the belt, that the tradition would come true. So, here I am at Malcolm's wedding all by myself in Tuscaloosa. I was looking around to see if I could spot anyone I knew and found Jason. I had not seen him in years and was excited to see someone I knew. We made small talk and he asked if I were married yet. I told him nope and that I did not plan on it either. About that time Malcolm announced he was throwing the garter. As it flew through the air, I noticed that it was headed in my direction. I told myself to step right and get out of the way.

Jason must have done the same because he stepped left. Both of our steps opened a large spot for the garter to land. He looked at me and I at him. We both had the same expression on our face that said, *"I'm not picking it up."* After a few awkward seconds, I thought about how awkward Malcolm must have felt. I guess I didn't want to disappoint him because I reached down and picked it up while stating the fact that I wasn't getting married anytime soon, especially since I didn't have a girlfriend. With confidence the old tradition would not prevail, I shoved it into my pocket and life went on as usual until the day Kori refused to rent a movie."

They all laughed after I told my story, and then I looked at my watch and realized it was time for me to go. "Well, guys, I hate to leave good company, but Tamika should be almost done changing, so I guess I need to be heading upstairs. I appreciate you all making the drive from Tuscaloosa for our wedding. Be careful going home."

Just about the time I had started up the steps, Brannon spoke up. "Hold on, before you go, you have got to tell them about the holes."

"Holes?" I asked him with a puzzled look on my face.

"I was telling them about how you had to dig holes before your wedding and they don't believe me."

With a little smirk on my face that said I can't believe it either, I walked back to the bar and I began to tell my story about holes. "I always knew that I could dig a hole. I have dug myself into holes with words that I spoke; I have dug some holes with machines, such as a backhoe and some I have dug with my actions. But today, on my wedding day, I dug holes with a shovel." Seeing that they were intrigued with my story, I kept going. "So, here I am, all dressed up in my tuxedo for my big day when I hear my dad yelling down the stairs.

'Cliff, get a shovel and go get some dirt to fill in some holes to keep people from falling.'

'Where am I supposed to get dirt, Dad?'

'I don't care where you get it from, I guess dig some holes in the woods. Just fill up the holes in the yard so guests don't trip and fall. I don't need a lawsuit on top of everything else!'

I could tell that my blood pressure was on the rise as I walked into the garage to look for a shovel. Thoughts raced through my mind during the trip to the woods. *Here it is my wedding day, and I have to go and dig a hole for dirt in my Tuxedo one hour before I am to be married. Guests will be arriving any moment, and I am out here with a shovel getting all sweaty digging up dirt to fill in holes. Why was this not thought about earlier this week, and out of all people, why am I the one digging the holes? Despite my frustration, I knew he was right, so I gathered the dirt and filled the holes in the yard to smooth out the foundation of the land which held our wedding.*

Guys, it's been fun, but it's time for me to grab Tamika and toss the garter. Maybe one of you will get lucky and catch it! Thank you again for making the trip." I turned away from my life as a single man and headed upstairs to begin my life as a married one.

———◆◆◆———

All throughout the Bible are scriptures regarding opening up the blind eyes. It wasn't until a year or two after becoming a Christian that I fully understood the meaning. I was blind to my thoughts and the meaning of filling up the holes that day. But now, I believe God used that labor to help me deal with the guilt I had created. With my eyes wide open and my deaf ears made new, I am now able to hear what God's whispering voice is telling me about the irony that was taking place.

Months before our wedding, Tamika and I had dug ourselves into a hole. It was a hole that was not in God's will, but through His grace we found peace. His blessings that took place on our wedding day were confirmation to us that we made the right decision to marry and by doing so I now believe that we had filled in the hole we dug and got back on the plan He had for us. We had chosen the correct gate.

Our First Child

இந

After I graduated in December of 1999, we moved to Tamika's home town of Florence, AL. There we found a nice apartment to begin our life together. I found a job that took me out of town fifty miles to Huntsville six days a week. I would report to work at nine o'clock a.m. dressed up in a suit and tie to convince shoppers that BMW was the Ultimate Driving Machine while Tamika was at home resting up for the delivery of our first child. My long hours began to wear on me as cabin fever began to wear on her. Fortunately, Tamika's family visited often and made sure she had a ride to her appointments if I was unable to make it.

She had to report to her gynecologist once a week to check the growth of our soon-to-be son. During the last checkup, she began to bleed, which is normal, but the bleeding did not stop, and the doctor decided it was time to induce. Phone calls were made, and visitors started to file in one by one. I was a bundle of nerves as the time was near for our first child to arrive. Not knowing what to expect, I listened carefully to all the advice that was given by the ones experienced in birthing a child.

"When you walk in, hold out your hand and ask for your epidural," the younger of her two sisters told her. At the time, I did not know what an epidural was, so I did not understand the wisdom that was just spoken. But after witnessing the increasingly, intensive pain she suffered following being induced to the lack of pain after the epidural, I decided her sister was a genius.

Before the epidural, I was not enjoying the look on Tamika's face during each contraction and wanted to move more towards the doctor. I had never witnessed anything so amazing before and didn't want to miss the exciting part. However, the grip Tamika had on my hand told me I was better off to stand by her and cheer her on.

Now, Tamika is a fighter, and for some reason, she tries to endure as much pain as she can before succumbing to any medicine for relief. The evidence of this was in the delivery room on Feb 2, 2000. She was strong while trying to avoid taking an epidural and suffered through a lot of pain to prove her strength. Honestly, to this day I don't understand why she put herself through what she did. I suppose that's just the way a barrel-racing, country girl is made. Nonetheless, even the toughest of the toughest have a breaking point, and Tamika found hers when the doctor looked up to inform her she was dilated seven centimeter. It was her last chance to receive the epidural.

At this time in my life, I was a twenty-three-year-old, ignorant young man who thought he had everything figured out, so when the doctor asked everyone to leave the room for the epidural procedure, I graciously declined. In my mind, an epidural was nothing more than local anesthesia, which would be administered as a shot in the middle lower region of my wife. It wasn't until the doctor denied my attempt to stay, followed by informing me exactly how and where the procedure was actually performed, that I decided to agree. I did not want to be any part of what was about to happen, and showed myself to the door.

I walked into the lobby to update our support team which consisted mostly of family, a few local friends and a Brannon who drove three hours from Tuscaloosa to get a glance when our son arrived. I was shocked to see him there and couldn't wait to go back in to let Tamika know. Time passed quickly as I caught up with Brannon and before I knew it, I was welcomed back into the room. As I approached her, I noticed a relaxed look on her face, which took me by surprise. "Tamika, are you feeling ok?"

"I'm fine. I just need to know when to push. I can't feel anything except a little pressure."

The doctor spoke up, "Don't push yet! Mr. Powell, would you like to watch as the head of your first child crowns?" Checking with Tamika to make sure she was ok, I left her side to catch a peak of the crowning of my sons head. I was amazed by what I saw and fixated on the delivery of our first child.

The next minute or two became very intense for me. Along with the head of my child appeared to be an arm that was trying to creep its way out. They appeared to be attached to one another and inside my head I began to panic.

What was I going to do? How do I tell Tamika? How many surgeries will it take? Oh my goodness, why is my son's arm growing out of his head!

Just about the time I completed my last thought, the rest of my son was delivered and all parts fell into place. I was so relieved and in awe of what I had just witnessed. The love I felt when I held my son in my arms for the first time was indescribable.

Over the next few days, Tamika and I enjoyed our child as well as learning about parenting. I watched the nurse give him his first bath, and I changed my first diaper. Everything was in place as should be except for one thing. Our son needed a name.

Throughout the entire pregnancy, Tamika knew that our son's name would be Peyton. I was against the name but did not push the issue. I was just hoping something would change her mind. Don't get me wrong, I don't have anything against the name Peyton except for the fact that at that time, the University of Alabama had been defeated in football for the past four years by Tennessee with a quarterback named Peyton. I did not want to go through my life being reminded of those horrible defeats each time I called my sons name, nor did I want people thinking he was named after a Tennessee quarterback.

Fortunately, my son was born with dark colored hair instead of the red hair my wife had pictured on a boy named Peyton. When the nurse came in for the second time asking for his name Tamika spoke up.

"We just cannot name him Peyton. Peyton was supposed to have red hair and his is dark."

"What should we name him?"

`"I don't know," Tamika replied as she reached for the baby name book.

The nurse informed us that we could think about it one more day, but she would need a name by tomorrow morning. We debated on every name in the boy baby name book we had purchased, but nothing seemed to fit. The name we did like was a name that I insisted we could not choose. We mulled over multiple ways of getting around using the exact name. We tried to change the "a" with an "e" which didn't work. Then, we decided we should replace an "n" with a "d" but that just didn't work either. So, we slept on it one more night.

The next morning we woke up with it heavy on our hearts. Tamika decided to justify what we both knew was the proper name for our son. The justification process was started by her saying, "You know Cliff, he did drive three and a half hours from Tuscaloosa to Florence, sat in the waiting room for hours upon hours only to miss the delivery by ten minutes."

I agreed; she had a good point. With the clock nearing midnight our friend Brannon decided he needed to get on the road due to a class exam he had at eight in the morning. I thought back to the events that played out just two nights before. I thought about how I hated he waited so long and would miss the delivery. But he was right; the three hour trip back to Tuscaloosa was not leaving him much time to sleep. So, when I learned he was leaving, I left Tamika's side for the second time in the delivery room to express my gratitude and bid him farewell.

A nurse walked in, which broke up my thought process, harshly stating, "If you don't have a name for this baby by the next time I come in, I'm naming him!"

"Cliff, he was there for us every time we needed him and helped us in a lot of ways." Tamika was convinced that our son would be named Brannon, but I was unsure of how this would affect our friend's ego.

"Tamika, you do know this will go to his head." I told her in a joking manner. "But you are right and I do like the name myself. Besides, anything is better than naming him after a quarterback from Tennessee."

"He deserves to get the big head. He has done a lot for us and I love the name, so Brannon it is." Tamika's mind was made up, and I knew in my heart, she was right.

The nurse walked in around mid-morning with a piece of paper. "Do I need to fill this in for you or have you decided on a name yet?"

Tamika took a quick look at me; then, back to the nurse she replied, "His name will be Brannon Taylor Powell."

Monte Sano

ᘒᘒ

The day after we left the hospital with Brannon, I went back to trying to earn money for our family. Since I was new to the job, I began studying all the brochures trying to learn as much as possible about the Ultimate Driving Machine. After a test drive with a coworker named Jim, I learned to put the brochure away and ask one question that would most likely determine the outcome. "Do you like to drive a car or do you like to ride in a car?"

The test drive Jim had taken me on was a thirty minute round trip up Monte Sano Mountain in Huntsville, AL. It was a pretty drive that was comprised of scenes overlooking the city. But I didn't carry clients up there for the view. I took them on the thirty minute trip to prove the car they were in was in fact the Ultimate Driving Machine. With forty-five degree turns and one ninety degree turn, which required most vehicles to slow down to a minimum of fifteen miles per hour, it was the perfect test drive that would push the car to its limits.

I drove that route enough times to become confident in knowing the car's ability before carrying my first customer on the route. I learned how to push the car through the turns and how to force the car to a point the Dynamic Stability Control, a safety feature to prevent the car from losing control, would activate. This was usually the deal maker or the deal breaker. It all depended on if the customer was honest when I asked my question prior to our test drive.

"Do you like to drive a car or do you like to ride in a car?" Usually, the customer would not completely understand, and I would go into a more detailed explanation of what I was asking. "A BMW is more of a driver's car and is really for someone that likes to take control of the road and push the limit. However, it also offers a comfortable ride for those not so aggressive drivers that just enjoy traveling down the road in a comfortable riding vehicle. So, are you a driver or a rider?" If the answer was rider then we would take a spin around the block and hit the interstate for a mile or two which offered the comfortable feel they were looking for. But if the answer was driver... it was on.

The trip for drivers would start out on the interstate, and I would walk them through how they could really take control of the car by switching it from automatic to manual by simply sliding over the gear shift into manual mode. We would then ease off the interstate and begin our trail up the mountain. Instructing them when to upshift, downshift and accelerate, I would take them on the ride of their life.

By the time we topped the mountain and came out of the ninety degree turn at a speed forty-five in a fifteen mph turn, the Dynamic Stability Control system would kick in. The driver would feel the car losing control and begin to panic, but I knew what was about to happen. The DSC system sent pulses to each brake individually which would regain control of the car, saving us from a major crash. When we stopped shortly after the turn, almost everyone would look at me and say, "Wow, what a car!" After walking them through what just happened, we would head back to the dealership while I went over the remaining safety features of the car. If they truly were a driver, they were signing up for a car that day. If not, they were very anxious to get back into their own car.

Sales started to climb, and my manager saw huge potential in me. She spoke about potential earnings and how life could be a lot better in the right place. Little did I know, she had an agenda behind the comments she was making. It wasn't until I learned that she was about to marry the Sales Manager at the BMW dealership in Birmingham that I began to piece it all together. Her time in Huntsville was ending soon and she was pushing for me to make the move as well.

The thought of moving Tamika away from her family made my stomach turn. Were we certain this was the right move? Absolutely not, but we were both convinced that I could be a lot more successful in Birmingham, especially since I would be selling Porsche, Audi, Lexus, and Range Rover as well as BMW. It was an impressive line up to me and I had high hopes.

So, in June of 2000, we said goodbye to our apartment in Florence and made the move that would begin a downward spiral in our marriage.

Sweet Tea

When I arrived at Tom Williams for my first day, I expected some big things. I had a lot of support in Huntsville and was anticipating the same. Unfortunately, the only advice I ever received was on my first day when my manager told me to go ahead and buy a house because I was going to make eighty thousand by the end of the year. I did not buy a house nor did I make the eighty thousand. In fact, I made less than I had in Huntsville, a lot less.

Frustrated and disappointed, I tried to figure out why I was not able to close as many deals as I did in Huntsville, and two things occurred to me. One was the reputation of the other salesmen. The second one was the missing mountain called Sano. I had searched and searched for a great place to demonstrate the cars' abilities, but there was nothing close enough to use. In the middle of downtown Birmingham, I was stuck with fighting traffic and straight roads. There was nothing for me to get excited about and no way to sell them on all the features I would mention. The other salesmen had been there for years and paid their dues. They had an established reputation that would bring in referrals and repeat business. I was left with joy riders that just wanted to test drive a high line vehicle or people that thought they could afford the cars but really could not.

I had made a bad decision, and life at home was evidence. However, getting me to admit a mistake back then was just not happening. I didn't understand how to be a great husband and was too full of pride to admit any of my faults. The stress of supporting a young family while in a job that paid on a straight commission pay scale was wearing on me. The sweet, carefree man Tamika married was turning into a chauvinistic self-centered man.

I remember the day I realized what I was becoming pretty well. It had been a frustrating day at work and self-pity had been building. As I walked in, I said hi to Tamika who was lying on the couch and walked over to the fridge. When I opened the door, I found an empty tea pitcher with only enough sweet tea left at the bottom to tease my taste buds. I took the pitcher into the living room while yelling, "Really, Tamika, can't you at least make some tea! I'm gone to work all freaking day and you are here drinking up the tea. The least you could do is not put the empty pitcher back into the fridge without making more? How hard is it to make tea? You take a pot out, boil some water, add sugar, add tea bags and stir then voila, TEA!!!!"

Promptly, Tamika chimed in letting me know real quick that she would never be making tea for me ever again! I really didn't take her seriously, but I also had not seen the strong side of my wife. I learned that day; Tamika was a woman of her word. I'm not really sure if it was due to the argument or just the fact that she can live without tea; nevertheless, it was thirteen years before she made tea again.

The fight with Tamika brought me to a realization that I had reached a point where the stress was too much, and it was time for us to make a change. I decided that I needed some advice and picked up the phone to call my dad. After listening to what I was going through and how selling high line vehicles was just not for me, he told me he had been considering hiring someone for a service advisor position and asked if I would come work for him.

Downward Spiral

✧

Dad was the third generation to own the small automotive repair shop in Cullman and had big dreams of expanding the business to multiple locations. Passing down what he hoped to be a financially stable business to his sons was a dream of his. The timing was right, and I was looking for a change. After talking it over with Tamika, six months after moving to Hoover, we decided to move to Cullman.

Cullman was a booming town that still managed to hold onto the small town feel. Crime was low, small businesses still had a chance to thrive, and the people were still friendly enough to lend a hand if you called on them. I was surprised at myself that I moved back home. When I had left Cullman in 1995, I swore that I would never move back. However, I also swore that I would never date again and wound up being married three short years later.

Tamika began working on finishing up her degree by enrolling in UAB during the spring semester of 2001. She had always battled having to leave Alabama early, but the longer she was enrolled at UAB, the more pride she found in their education program. It took Tamika a while to fall in love with Cullman, which in her eyes was inferior to her home town of Florence. However, just like UAB, the longer she stayed, the more she found to love, especially one particular school where she hoped to teach one day.

During her final semester in 2002, Tamika was assigned to student teach under a second grade teacher. She fell in love with not only the students but the school and all who worked there. Fortunately, she happened to be paired with a teacher that was completing her final semester prior to retiring, which meant there would be an open position for the following year. When the job became available, Tamika applied and with high recommendations became the newest teacher in second grade. She was very happy and now had a reason to want to live in Cullman. I was thankful for her new position as I was afraid that if she was not able to find a job in Cullman, she would begin to push to move back home.

Throughout the rest of the year, Tamika adjusted to teaching second grade, and I was promoted to shop manager, which came along with a nice pay raise. Brannon was into his terrific two's and our latest addition "Bauchser" was a lab in his puppy stage. Life was getting hectic, but we enjoyed every minute of it. Financially, we were saving and started investing to increase our net worth. Up until the move to Cullman, our life had been a struggle. However, with two steady jobs and a balanced budget, Tamika and I were finally getting ahead. But what we didn't know was we were about to begin the downward spiral that led to opening one wrong gate after another.

At the end of the school year, all non-tenured teachers received a pink slip. Tamika had poured her heart and soul into her first year so when she was let go, it hit hard. Life sometimes doesn't seem fair and we struggle to find reason, but with time if you have opened your eyes to see God working, you can eventually find Him bringing it all to His Glory. Unfortunately, during the time she lost her job, my eyes were blind to God's way, and all I knew to do at the time was tell her I was sorry and to hang in there, which is nothing but mere words. Looking back now, I should have been praying for her strength along with our obedience to accept God's will.

During the summer, Tamika worked hard to find a new job, but it just never seemed to work out. Tamika was very passionate about teaching, and the thought of not finding a job was too much to bear. As the 2003-2004 school year began, she reached the point of giving up. I could tell she was concerned about our finances and rightfully so. We had just bought a new house, had one child and recently learned that we had another on the way. I tried to encourage her and told her everything would be fine. I had a solid job that was going to provide enough money for us to survive. But then again, I had no idea what life had in store for us just around the corner.

Just like the heat of the summer is replaced with the cold of winter, all things change. Tamika learned this through an eggshell on a special Valentine's Day and again through a heartbreaking job loss years later. In November 2003, I learned about a change that would affect our life for years. It was a Tuesday morning when dad walked into the shop office and told me to not take in any more business, he was closing the doors. After a 61 year run, our family business was coming to an end leaving my family without any household income for the first time since we married.

My dad was great friends with the local Tool Group (TG) tool dealer who had been calling on the shop for over fifteen years. Just a few months before dad closed for business, I had met with the tool dealer and his manager for lunch to discuss the possibility of me becoming a Franchisee. He appeared to make a good living, and I was considering giving it a try.

After dad closed the shop, I reached out to dad's friend and another interview was lined up. I learned about a trial program TG had implemented to attract younger adults into the business. After talking it over with two other men in the program, I became more confident that this was a smart move. Tamika agreed with me, so I decided to give it a try. A contract was signed, and a brand new eighteen foot long tool truck was delivered to my house and shortly after came the goodies.

Boxes upon boxes of new TG tools began to appear at my doorstep every other day. It was like Christmas for a man every week at my house only these gifts came with a hefty tool bill. The first year in business proved to be a success as I made a large profit and had gained trust from most of my customers. Being reliable and having high demand items in stock went a long way to my success. I felt that I was finally on my way to becoming the household provider I had dreamed about.

At the end of the year, I had the option to walk away with the equity I had built in my business and end my career with them or sign up to become a full time dealer. The decision was difficult and I contacted many people for wisdom but the one I should have spoken to was never contacted. The feeling in my gut told me to not sign the papers but I ignored it and chose a gate that led down another wrong path. If I would have only understood the way God spoke back then, I would have known my gut was His words telling me that I was about to choose the wrong gate. That's what happens when you are not in a relationship with Christ. His whispers fall on deaf ears leaving behind missed opportunities that allow us to walk down the right path.

Our Second Child

cn

I was in my first month as a TG Trial Franchisee when our first daughter was born. One of my customers and I were standing in the long walking aisle of my truck. Surrounding the aisle were shelves covered with tools. Above where we stood were tools strapped to the ceiling. The tool truck was a man's candy store. I knew if I could engage my customers in a discussion long enough, their eyes would begin to wander which always led to them making a purchase before exiting the truck. The topic of discussion on this day was my wife's pregnancy. My customer asked, "Is she having a boy or a girl?"

"It's going to be a girl," I replied while a smile of pride crept onto my face.

"That's great! I have a girl and two boys of my own and I'm telling you what, I love my boys, but there is just something about the girl. When she looks into your eyes for the first time, your heart will just melt," he said as he began to step off the truck. "Best of luck to you and your wife; I hope all goes well."

———◆———

Luck was what I believed in back then. "I guess I am lucky," I would say as great things happened in my life. But what I viewed as luck then, I now view as a blessing from God. Within a couple of weeks of starting my business, Tamika and I were at her doctor's for a scheduled visit and learned some news that our baby was not growing, which brought concern to the doctor.

"I recommend that we induce," Tamika's doctor told us.

"Really? It's two weeks from her due date. Is it safe to induce that early?" I asked the doctor just to help calm my nerves.

"Since there are no signs of growth, it is possible that something may be wrong, which leaves us with the following options:

1. Deliver the baby so we can determine what that is and help her.
2. Continue to wait and risk a potential still birth.

We cannot treat the baby inside her belly, so I am encouraging the both of you to agree to induce early so we can determine if something is wrong."

After the doctor provided us with the options, we both agreed it was best to induce. We set up the appointment and went home to prepare to bring home our baby girl. I was on cloud nine and could not wait to see my little girl.

We arrived at Cullman Regional Medical Center at 6:00 a.m. and Tamika started receiving the medicine that would begin the contractions an hour later. By 11:00 a.m. she had delivered our beautiful daughter, Mandolyn. As I leaned over to kiss Tamika I told her, "She's beautiful and you're amazing. I am so proud of you."

The pediatrician arrived thirty minutes later and gave her a clean bill of health. "Congratulations, she's great," he said as he left the room. Tamika and I looked at each other with pride and replied.

"Thank you."

I walked over to our new daughter and picked her up to take a better look at her. Brannon, who was about to turn four at the time, entered the room and wanted to hold her. As I helped him hold his little sister, my mom noticed that she was making a strange noise, which sounded a lot like a little grunt. I blew it off as baby noises and said, "Okay, Brannon, let me see her now." Selfishly, I took her from him after only a minute or two. For some reason, I could not stand to be away from Mandolyn very long at all. At the time, I thought I was just in awe with the fact that I had a baby girl, now I realize it was God trying to alert me as to what was going on. A daughter should be safest in her father's arms, but my ears were deaf and my eyes were blind to what He was telling me. Thoughts of the noises she was making never crossed my mind.

It had been five hours since the doctor issued a clean bill of health, and the light from the window no longer illuminated our room as well as it had throughout the day. Tamika was in and out of sleep throughout the day, and I was selfishly holding Mandolyn telling Tamika that I would bring her over in a minute. About that time, I noticed the color of her skin seemed darker than usual and asked Tamika what she thought. She agreed and mentioned how dark she looked, but neither of us made a connection as to why she was much darker than Brannon at his birth. As the sun was setting, the room became darker and darker which camouflaged just how blue our daughter had become leaving us unaware of the danger our daughter was in.

Another thirty minutes had passed before a nurse walked in. She immediately noticed the color of our daughter as well as the noises. "How long has she been this color?"

"I don't really know, as the sun was setting, the room grew darker and that's when we noticed I guess."

"What about the grunting noise? How long has it been going on?"

"My mom noticed it shortly after lunch I guess. Why?"

Without answering me, the nurse left the room at a pace that was faster than normal. It wasn't twenty seconds before another nurse walked in and said, "You're right, you're right!"

Before I knew it, she grabbed my daughter out of my arms and sped out the door leaving Tamika and me both frozen staring into one another's eyes. "What was that about?" I asked.

"I don't know, Cliff, but you need to follow her to see where she took my baby and find out what's going on!"

Hearing the urgency in Tamika's voice, my heart began to pound. I'm not sure if it was out of frustration, fear, anger or just the thought that my baby girl was taken away from me and I had no clue where she was. I approached the nurses' station and in an upset tone asked, "Where is my daughter?" The nurse apologized to me for the circumstance and requested that I put on a gown, mask and head bonnet so I could see my little girl.

As I walked through the double swinging doors into the nursery, I saw Mandolyn under an oxygen hood and a digital number lit in red, which stirred up a question. "What is fifty-five and what's going on?"

The nurse that grabbed her from me spoke up. "I'm sorry that I startled you, but in a circumstance like this, we cannot waste a single second."

"What circumstance?" I asked as if I really didn't want to hear her answer.

"Mr. Powell, your baby was blue. Fifty-five is her SAT rate or oxygen level. This tells us how much oxygen a person has in their bloodstream. The number should be in the upper nineties if not one hundred. Mr. Powell, the sounds you have been hearing has been your daughter gasping for air."

Stunned by the news I had just heard, I slowly turned around and headed away from the nursery. I walked down the hall and wondered how I was going to tell Tamika knowing she was going to be devastated.

Before entering the room, tears began to pour down my face. I hesitated to open the door and tried to gain composure. I didn't want Tamika thinking the worst, and as of right now Mandolyn was alive and receiving the oxygen she needed to keep her alive, so I decided to pass on opening the door that led me to Tamika. Instead, I went to the men's room to clear my face and regain composure.

Once I felt like I was strong enough to face Tamika without crying, I headed out of the bathroom and back to our room. Opening the door, I could see my wife's beautiful face that normally held a lovely smile that had turned into sadness. "You have been gone a long time."

As I sat down next to my wife, I could see the streaks of tear stains on her face, which told me she had been crying for a long time. I hurt for my wife and understood the pain. I tried to gather my composure in an attempt to be strong and proceeded to tell her what I had learned.

"What does this mean?" Tamika asked me.

"I don't know exactly. Let's just wait and see what the pediatrician says, but I'm sure everything will be okay, so let's try not to think the worst."

With a nod of her head showing her agreement, she replied, "I want to go see Mandolyn." Still in pain but able to walk, she was determined to get out of bed to see her daughter. Tamika is strong willed, allowing nothing to hold her down when her mind is set, so although I felt like she needed to rest, I understood and helped her to her feet. Together we traveled the short distance to the nursery with a long, slow walk leaving a trail of concerned tears along our path. When we arrived, Mandolyn looked helpless under the oxygen hood and Tamika just stood there, crying. I held my wife closely trying to provide her with security while telling her everything would be fine.

Shortly after we entered, the pediatrician walked in and said, "What happened? I just saw this baby this morning and she checked out fine." The nurses proceeded to explain the situation followed by him turning towards us to discuss the plan. With gentleness, the doctor explained to us that he wanted to observe her overnight to see if she would progress. If she could maintain a healthy SAT rate on her own, then, she would stay. If not, then, she would be transferred to a hospital in Birmingham first thing in the morning.

I barely slept a wink that night. All I could think about was how I had no control over the situation. I knew that if I could not control the outcome of my daughter, hopefully, God could. After lying in the recliner for what seemed to be hours, I decided to ask God to take control and begged Him for the life of my daughter. It was the first time I had prayed in a long time. When the morning came and the pediatrician made his rounds, I realized that I must have fallen asleep shortly after my prayer, which surprised me. Before the prayer, I was not able to rest at all. The horrible thoughts of losing a child kept me up almost all night. But I somehow found rest shortly after my quick prayer. I know now that's the way God works; He takes our burdens and gives us rest.

It was rest that I needed as the news the doctor provided us when he walked in was not what we had hoped. "Hey, guys, she needs to be transferred to a hospital that has a NICU. We have a couple of options on where to send her. I have experience at both and can validate that they are both wonderful places. Treatment will be excellent no matter which you choose; however, the NICU visitation rules are very different. The first option is to go to Kid's First Hospital where you would be limited to visiting hours throughout your stay. The second option is to go to St Martin's Hospital. There they would allow you to stay with her as much as you like. It's up to you, but I need a decision now."

Tamika was not willing to leave her side, so the choice was simple. We packed up and left for the hour long trip to St. Martin's Hospital. During the trip, I began searching for answers to questions that had been weighing on my mind. I was not deeply rooted in Christ and did not understand the spiritual world or the word faith. All I understood at the time was the word fear, and that is exactly what I had. I was in fear that my daughter was not going to make it. Being the solution provider of the house, I was used to fixing everything. But this time was different. I had no idea as to what to do or how to fix this.

However, Tamika was strong and brought the balance we needed. "Cliff, you just need to turn to God and pray. Don't just pray once... pray often. I have been praying ever since the nurse took Mandolyn from you and now feel confident that God has placed strength in our daughter, and she is going to be okay."

I was a critic by nature who analyzed everything, so when it came to belief, I simply couldn't rationalize it. All I knew was that my daughter was being admitted to the NICU at a major hospital in the largest city in Alabama, and only one thought kept passing through my mind. My daughter is on the brink of death ...

When we arrived at the NICU room, I immediately found Mandolyn. Wires were running from all parts of her body and the tubes that ran up her nose and down her throat looked as if she was in a battle, fighting to stay alive. I was distraught with sadness at the sight of my baby girl. But as my eyes began to wander around the room, I realized some of her roommates were much less fortunate.

At that time, we were the only parents in the NICU, so I took advantage of it and began to walk around the room. As I approached the first crib, I saw a baby that was the size of a large squirrel. I searched for the tag on the crib that would tell me the baby's birth weight. My eyes were opened to how blessed we were that Mandolyn at 5lb 10oz was twice the size of this baby. I asked the nurse how the baby was doing. "He is doing great. Actually, his brother was able to go home last week. That's why his parents are not here today."

"His brother?"

"Yes, he is one of three. His other brother did not survive"

In the corner of the NICU was a small room that caught my eye. I approached the room that was sealed off with a glass wall and door that appeared to be specially made just for the space. Inside the wall was a smaller wall that resembled a closet without a door. Inside the closet area hung specialty gowns and masks with gloves that were different from other gloves I had ever seen in any other hospital.

"Ma'am, do you mind telling me a little bit about this room?"

"It is an isolation room that holds all of our extremely critical babies."

After seeing one of the triplets in the crib, I was in shock that she was now referring to a baby that could have more complications than what I had already seen. Curiously, I asked if there was a baby in the room now.

"Yes. He is very sensitive, and we have to dress in the special garments before entering his crib area. I can't say much more than that."

I was now taken aback and began to walk over to Mandolyn until I noticed another couple had just walked in and found their way to the crib that held their son. I walked over and asked them their names along with how their son was doing. The father looked down at their son, and I could tell it was hard for him to share. "He was born with a defective heart and has already undergone two heart surgeries. Thankfully, both have gone well. But he still has three more to go. One next week and then if it is successful another at the age of three and a final surgery at the age of five."

I'm sure the look on my face told them, but I wanted to speak it. "I'm so sorry to hear this. I hope everything turns out okay." As I walked away I could not help but feel a heavy burden for them but also felt a sense of relief about to our situation.

"Tamika, have you looked around? We have the healthiest baby in here."

Taking a moment to look away from Mandolyn while gazing around the room, she replied, "I have and it just breaks my heart.

I can't imagine how all of these babies' parents are coping. I know that we are in good hands here and she is going to be okay." Tamika gave me some confidence with her words. However, when the NICU doctor finally made his rounds, my confidence took a brief turn for the worse.

The Treatment Plan

♪♫

When the doctor came in to tell us Mandolyn's diagnosis of Premature Lung Disease and treatment plan, I was confused and needed some clarification. "I don't understand. She was not premature. She was thirty eight weeks when my wife was induced. Are you saying this could have been avoided had we not induced?"

"That depends on why the decision was made to be induced early."

"Tamika had been measuring small with no indications of growth for a couple of weeks. It was recommended that we deliver the baby ASAP just in case there was something wrong. The gynecologist told us it is much better to have her delivered and treatable than to be still in the womb where she cannot be treated."

"To me and what I have seen in the past, she looks more like a thirty four week old baby, which can easily be missed. When the gestational age is determined, there is always a plus or minus two to three week window. With that said, I think your gynecologist was accurate in the decision to induce early, and we are now at the treatment part you mentioned."

Stepping back to absorb what he had just said, I realized that he was right. Tamika's gynecologist was dead on. If it had not been for her inducing Tamika, we may have lost our daughter. It's amazing how we were warned about conditions such as these prior to delivery. However, we were caught up in the drama of our situation and had forgotten everything Tamika's gynecologist had told us. I was thankful for the reminder and grew even more confident in Tamika's choice of doctor.

The prognosis for Mandolyn was high. The plan was to keep her in the NICU for at least ten days to monitor her lungs while she was kept under an oxygen hood until they were able to wean her off. She would then graduate to another bed and begin the stage in which we would become more involved by changing diapers and bathing her. "The process will seem long and tiring as she will show signs of improvement by coming off the hood but will go right back on it so be prepared as it is normal," the doctor warned us as he left the room.

Tamika spoke up right before the door closed, "What about the feeding tubes? I would like for her to nurse if possible."

"Once she begins to maintain a proper SAT rate for a length of time, she can come out of the hood temporarily and try to nurse or at least take the milk from the bottle. We strongly believe that mommy's milk helps them heal." Tamika now had something to focus on.

Being caught up in all the action, I had not realized that Tamika had not had an opportunity to hold Mandolyn since the first hour of her birth. She was too worn out after the delivery and slept most the day right up to the minute the nurse grabbed her from me. She was anxious to get to hold her and stayed in a rocking chair by her side every night and day just waiting for the opportunity.

Two Sundays had gone by before the day rolled around when Mandolyn was well enough to be held. I remember walking in the NICU from my workday and seeing a glow on Tamika's face. I gave her a kiss and asked, "Why the big smile?"

"I got to hold Mandolyn today!"

"You did!"

"Yes, when I spoke to her for the first time, she smiled as if saying, 'There's that voice I have been hearing for the past nine months.' It felt so good to hold her, Cliff. I didn't want to put her down."

"I have to admit, Tamika, I'm jealous, but I'm happy that you were able to hold her."

"I can't wait to take her home."

"I can't wait either, Tamika. That day will come. Hopefully it will come soon."

The day to take our baby home came a lot sooner than we had even hoped. I believe that Mandolyn being held by her mom as well as being able to nurse gave her strength as she progressed rapidly from that moment on. Within four to five days, our daughter was healed, and we were headed home!

A Second Chance

♪♪

I was far from being a follower of Christ, but the couple of weeks Mandolyn spent in the NICU brought me closer to God. Tamika was already spirit filled, but I was just learning a little bit of what His blessing could bring. With the conditions that came with the birth of Mandolyn, Tamika began to realize the plan God had for her. I was not easily convinced as I would refer to it as happenstance. However, knowing what I know now, I'm convinced He freed her up to enable her to be where she needed to be during the first eight months of Mandolyn's life.

The time they spent together was priceless, and although she missed teaching, Tamika was thankful to be unemployed. But by the time summer rolled around, Tamika knew it was time to get back to her calling as a teacher. She began the interview process; and over the two month summer break, she did not receive any offers. Her heart ached, and she began to wonder if she was really meant to teach. Even though she had realized why she lost her job a year ago and was thankful for the time with her daughter, she was still human, and the love for her old school made her ache with a longing to return to teaching. She would often pray, asking God to help her be patient and wait for His timing. She realized that God's will for her life was a far more superior plan than our will and the position she was meant to receive would eventually surface. But when?

I was going on my ninth month as a Trial Franchisee for the Tool Group when Tamika received the call she had been praying for.

It was the new principal at the school where Tamika had formerly taught. She had called to inform Tamika about an opportunity for a third grade position. Instantly, all of her pain and suffering seemed to be replaced with joy and happiness as she felt in her spirit that it was the answer to her prayers. After the interview was over, Tamika received one more call which confirmed that she once again would be teaching at the school she had loved so much.

"Yes, I am very interested. Thank you so much. I cannot tell you how much this means to me." Tamika hung up the phone and began calling for me. "Cliff … Cliff! You will never believe this. Where are you Cliff?" Tamika ran outside and slung open the door on my tool truck. As I looked up, I noticed the tears rolling down her face and began to get the lump in my throat expecting horrible news. But that lump was soon replaced by a smile as she told me all about the conversation that had just taken place with a person that we refer to as the angel sent to us from God.

A Hidden Gem

⁓

Three months before we decided to look for a house, Tamika and I had dinner plans with another married couple. When we pulled into their driveway, they were walking out the door to take some teenagers to a campout. Since we were riding with them to the restaurant, we decided to ride with them to the campout and leave from there. As we entered the gravel road that led to the campout, I noticed it was the road that had always made me curious. "I have passed by this road so many times throughout my life and have always wondered what was down here," I informed everyone in the car.

Two hundred yards down the gravel drive nestled back in the woods was a beautiful two story home along with acres upon acres of open land perfect for horses or cattle. Who would have thought that this house was just minutes from all the schools and shopping of downtown Cullman. As we got out of the car, Tamika stood next to me turned to look at the house and said, "I sure hope we can live in a place like this one day."

"You never know, Tamika. Sometimes things happen. I never thought I'd be married to someone like you, but I am, and just like you … it's a hidden gem."

In February 2005, we celebrated Mandolyn's first birthday and Brannon's fifth. Seeing that we were quickly running out of space, we decided to get prequalified for a mortgage and begin our search for a new home. We looked at house after house for at least a month. All of them were either not our style, needed too much work or not in a good location. We wanted to stay on the East side close to Tamika's work and preferred the historical district. All of the houses we liked were out of our price range by fifty thousand or more. Tamika had always wanted a fixer upper as she had learned from her sister and brother in law that flipping houses could be very profitable. She searched and searched for an old beat up house that was cheap and had potential.

"Cliff ... Cliff ... I found one!" Tamika, not knowing I was in the garage, was searching throughout the house looking for me. After finding me she said, "I have been hollering for you. Guess what? I found one!"

"You found what?"

"A house that needs a lot of work!"

"Tamika, I don't know. I just don't think we are ready to take on a complete remodel. We have two little kids that would get into everything. I think it is just too big of a risk."

With each failed attempt at finding a new home, things were already tense around our house. Knowing that we were not going to see eye to eye on this, I anticipated an argument. Unfortunately, I was right, and the argument became pretty intense, which led to her leaving for Florence with the kids for the rest of the weekend. For the first time in our marriage, I was concerned about the word divorce.

I spent the next thirty hours alone thinking about what we needed to do to get back in agreement. The only solution I had was to increase our budget for a new home and make a move that we could both be happy with. When Tamika walked through the door, I gave her a hug and told her I was sorry. I waited until the timing was right to present my new idea to her, and when it was time, I was relieved to know we were once again walking in unison.

Tamika was anxious to move and didn't hesitate to look in the latest real estate book for our new home. Our new price range opened up the market for us and as she glanced over each page, she could not believe what she came across.

"Cliff, it's the house that's hidden close to Pinewood. You know, the hidden gem. I want to go see it today if possible."

"Really?"

"Yes, Cliff. Call our agent and see if we can look at it today."

An appointment was set up for that afternoon, and we fell in love with it immediately. It turned out to be the house of a friend of my moms who was not living there anymore. Unknown to us, my mom's friend was in the middle of a divorce and her ex-husband needed to get out from underneath the payment. Tamika and I needed to find a buyer or a renter before we could be approved, so we worked out an agreement to swap houses in effort to make the deal come together. We were purchasing his and he was renting ours for a year with an agreement that we could sell ours anytime. In April of 2005, just a few months after Tamika and I stood in the same spot we stood the night of the campout and stared at our house which we once considered a hidden gem.

A Pivotal Moment

cJℓ

As you have turned from page to page, you have learned that I was everything except a true follower of Jesus Christ. I had friends all around me that were, but I never really connected with them all that well. To be honest, I never understood why they would give up what the world had to offer just for someone that may or may not have existed. However, in December of 2005, a glimpse of hope appeared to me during a time when our community was mourning the loss of a friend who spent his life chasing Jesus.

Whit Warren had a personality that could light up any room. Finding the best in every situation, to me, was an addiction Whit seemed to battle. However, it was a battle that did not need to be broken. But, there was another battle in Whit's life that did. Whit was plagued by seizures nearly all of his life, which is something he learned to overcome. However, following a night of worshipping Jesus at an event in Birmingham, Alabama, Whit's life silently ended in his bedroom during a seizure.

As thousands mourned for days over Whit's passing, I began searching my heart for why I was actually happy for him. When I realized it was his relationship with Jesus that warmed my heart, a glimpse of hope came over me. I will never forget the moment my life began to turn around.

I was standing on the front porch of my house sharing stories with friends about how Whit brought joy to each of us when it hit me that Whit was where he longed to be. I felt very sorry for Whit's family and loved ones but could not bring myself to feel sorry for Whit. Back then, I could not explain it all as I did not understand my feelings myself. But now that I too chase God, I truly understand the joy in my heart. Ecclesiastes 7:1 NIV tells us "A good name is better than fine perfume, and the day of death better than the day of birth," and my friend Whit had a great name. It was a name that came up a lot the night a group of us came together in memory of Whit's life.

The stories we all shared brought laughter and joy in a time of remembrance. Especially the one story I could not resist telling. It was a night around Christmas time that we visited my friend Brannon for dinner at his dad's house. Whit was there, and my son was in his *"terrible"* two's. It must have been a full moon that night as he was in rare form. Running throughout the house, my son Brannon was getting a little too rambunctious and Whit must have picked up on our failed efforts to settle him down. As Brannon turned a corner with curly hair blown back by the wind he created with his speed and grinning from ear to ear, Whit stopped him by saying, "Hey, boy! Do you see this belt on my waist?" My son's grin faded, but knowing Whit like we did, Tamika and I couldn't help but grin as Whit proceeded.

"Don't make me take it off and use it on your bottom. You hear me?"

The look on Brannon's face was priceless as he just tucked his head and walked to the chair we had instructed him to sit in many times before the altercation. Whit looked up at us and grinned, "I think I might have really scared him. I feel horrible. Maybe I should go and apologize."

"No, oh no don't really, don't. He deserved that. We have been trying for a while now to get him under control, and we applaud you," Tamika said as she was very happy to have her sanity back.

About a month after the dinner at my friend's house, we were sitting in the balcony of St. John's Church trying to enjoy the morning service. Brannon was once again in a mood to not sit still. He stood then sat, then would stand and sit again. This happened over and over until he reached a point that he wanted to go down to the lower floor and see his granny who was singing in the choir. Brannon must have spotted her from the distance and was determined to go to sit with her. Once the singing ended and the sermon began, Tamika and I were hopeful the desires to sit with Granny would fade. But, he was determined and everyone in the sanctuary was aware of it, including Whit who had made his way to a seat about three rows behind us. When Brannon decided to make a run for the door, I turned and noticed the eye contact he had made with Whit.

My friend looked down and tapped his belt three times. Brannon once again tucked his head in silence and humbly walked back to his seat. Not a peep was heard from him the remaining forty-five minutes of the service.

The stories kept on and on as Whit brought so much life to the people around him. Stories of Whit dressing up in a tuxedo with slick hair for a driver's license photo were told. The time he owned a monkey and the time he showed up at school with a fake i.d. were all considered classic. Whit had no use for a fake i.d. as he did not drink, but being a tall white skinny sixteen-year-old, there was humor to be found in the license of an old, obese African American woman that he presented as his fake i.d. Even to this day, I can see him as if he were coming up to me now asking me, "Do you think it will work, Cliff?" as he showed it to me in the gym my senior year. Whit always brought a smile to my face.

<hr>

You may be saying to yourself, this is crazy, why would the day of death be better than the day of birth? If you told this to me prior to 2008, I would have viewed it as crazy too. But now that I chase Jesus, I get it. You see this world we live in is so temporary that we must not take it for granted. Compared to eternity, our life is a mere blink of time. It's what comes after death that truly matters. If you live for Christ and walk with Him daily then what is there to fear. Definitely not death, as the Bible tells us in Ecclesiastes 4:2 "And I declared that the dead, who had already died, are happier than the living, who are still alive." If this is true, which I know that it is, then we must treat it as such. For this is the reason I found happiness in the midst of a sad and tragic loss.

I knew that my friend Whit is with Jesus and I wanted what Whit had. I was eager to learn more and more about how he could chase after something that was not tangible. This was a pivotal moment in my life and it took me many steps, along with a lot of backsliding, to get to where I am today. But, without the death of a young man named Whit who lived his entire life as a true disciple of Jesus Christ I would not be who I am today. *"Thank you Jesus for allowing Whit Warren to be a part of my life."*

Our Third Child

ઌ

In April of 2005, we moved for what we thought would be our last time. A large yard, land for horses, privacy, a large front porch, two outside landings on the back and one medium size back porch that sat just outside the sunroom where Tamika enjoyed growing plants and flowers. Outside of a basement, we thought it had everything we ever wanted.

I used the sunroom to take naps while lying on the rod iron swing we inherited from my Mamma and Pappa. It was a swing that I loved to nap in as a child while I was visiting my grandparents. Now, as an adult, I still enjoy that swing and the way it takes me back to a time when life was simple. The swing was positioned to look out the sunroom windows into the area where the kids, a swing set, and trampoline were kept. Life was good and we were enjoying our new home.

Tamika had always wanted a large family, and five was the number she had in mind. She had mentioned this to me several times, and I had always thought she was a little over her head. But like any man, I was willing to try as much as she wanted. Mandolyn's second birthday rolled around, and Tamika realized that something was missing. She always wanted our second and third child to be born within two years of each other and time was ticking. With her goal in mind and time working against us … let's just say that it didn't take long before Tamika was pregnant. I was not expecting this happen as fast as it did, but our third child was on her way.

It is strange how things happen in cycles sometimes. When Tamika was pregnant with Brannon, she was sick all the time and battled kidney stones. With Mandolyn, she was not nearly as sick and did not have the first sign of kidney stones. Her third pregnancy was just like the first, only this time, Tamika had a full time job teaching third grade.

Tamika battled morning sickness that lasted almost all day every day, along with three rounds of kidney stones. What impressed me the most was the fact that she still managed to teach almost every day up until the day before she was induced. The only times she missed was due to her being in the hospital for kidney infections that developed from the stones.

After school let out for the summer, Tamika spent most of her days by a pool trying to keep cool from being pregnant during one of the hottest summers Alabama had ever seen. I spent my days peddling tools off my tool truck trying to earn money to pay the bills.

The time was nearing for the birth of our third child, and we were both anxious for her arrival. "I can't wait until she is born, Cliff."

"I know, Tamika. It's exciting isn't it."

"Yes, it is. Do you think she will have red hair?"

"I don't know; I thought all of our children would but was wrong on the first two."

"Oh, I hope she does. I have always wanted a red-headed little girl."

"This time next week we will find out. We need to get some sleep. I have a busy day tomorrow. Goodnight." I gave her a kiss and rolled over to and fell asleep.

The next week flew by fast. Tamika was teaching, I was working and time was speeding up every day. Life was already hectic and I started to imagine how much more hectic it was about to become. The night before Tamika was to be induced life becoming more hectic was not the only thing on my mind.

After tossing and turning for a few minutes, I decided to speak up and see if I could ease my mind. "Tamika, are you nervous?"

"I am a little."

"Me too."

The time we had spent in the NICU with Mandolyn brought a new fear into our life.

"The way I see it, Cliff, is God's in control, and it is out of our hands. All we can do is pray that He will protect us."

"I agree."

Back then I really did not know how to pray all that well, and I always felt like a fool when I would pray. I was definitely not about to pray out loud so that she could hear me. I was still living the lifestyle that I wanted to live. A life full of worldly wants and earthly desires. I was also still drinking like a college student from time to time. So in place of the prayer that should have happened that night, we kissed each other goodnight and went to sleep.

When the alarm clock went off, Tamika nearly hopped out of bed. "Get up, I'm ready to get this baby out of me!" she said in a loving but demanding way. I took a quick shower, grabbed our bags and we headed out the door. As we made the turn in the driveway that gave us a good look at the front of our house, thoughts of pulling back into the drive as a family of five ran through my head.

By now, Tamika knew the routine. She walked in and changed out of her clothes and into the gown while asking the nurse for an epidural.

"Done this before, hun?" the nurse asked. We just laughed and kept prepping for the next few hours, which would prove that Tamika was a champ when it came to delivering babies as her doctor claimed.

"Tamika, you're a pro and should consider giving birthing classes. If all deliveries could be like this, my job would be a breeze," the doctor told her while leaving the room.

Our newborn baby girl was just as beautiful as our other two. With the exception of her hair, they all looked very similar. Brannon and Mandolyn were born with a lot of hair; number three was born with a very thin and very light in color head of hair.

"Cliff, she is going to be a red head. I just know it." Tamika's voice was full of excitement. She finally had the red-headed girl she had always wished for.

Tamika and I had been researching names since the day we learned about the pregnancy. If the baby was a boy, we had decided on Hodges. If the baby was a girl, we always knew she would be named Lillyann. The middle name was in question. We loved the name Hodges and it seemed appropriate since it was Tamika's mom's maiden name, but it just didn't seem to fit when she was born. We went back and forth on the topic a lot and finally decided on Tamika's middle name Reshea.

On the third day after delivery, our beautiful red-haired baby girl, Lillyann Reshea Powell was loaded into her infant seat, and we headed home. As I pulled back into the driveway and made the turn that gave us the good look at the front of our house, a tear ran down my face. I was proud to bring home my family of five.

Mini Cooper

❧

A few months after Lillyann was born, my business began to take a turn for the worse. The economy drastically decreased the ability to collect from customers that owed me money. Without their payments I was unable to meet the demands of my tool bill. Keeping my bill low enough to maintain inventory and meet the clients demand for special orders became more challenging than ever. If you remember, having enough inventory to keep your clients satisfied played a large role in maintaining a successful business. So, when I was on hold it was a huge deal and needed immediate attention. Efforts in returning slow moving items fell short most of the time. To my disappointment, when I was able to get my bill low enough I would be hit with products that meant little to my bottom line. The disappointment in my customer's eyes when they would ask if there tool came in was discouraging. The pride of pulling on the lot as the best tool dealer was now being replaced with shame and humility.

The route I used to run weekly was slowly being replaced with driving in and out of my territory trying to collect money from customers that had moved into another area. I was not providing the service my good customers deserved and became frustrated to be spending more time hunting down the ones who skipped out on their bill than I was on selling. On the flip side, I was becoming more and more wary about selling anything to anyone on the buddy system. Business was making a turn for the worse and my backorder log was evidence. I could not afford to pay my high tool bill, and when the price of diesel fuel went from one dollar and some change to over four dollars within months, I knew it was time to consider making a career change. Although business was getting tight, I was still willing to hold on a little longer – I didn't want to be seen as a quitter. I told myself I just needed a break. If I could come across a large sum of money to pay down on my bill, I could get off hold and get business running in the black again.

In January of 2007, I was supposed to attend a Kickoff banquet TG held yearly, but instead I skipped it for the Monster Truck Jam that I had promised to take the kids to months before the kickoff date was set. Brannon, Mandolyn and I were standing outside the Birmingham Jefferson Civic Center waiting for the doors to open at the Monster Truck Jam, when my phone rang. *Great, it's my zone manager. I wonder what she wants.* She was at the banquet and called to let me know that I had just won a brand new Mini Cooper.

"Do I have to be present to win?" I asked her knowing that I could be there within two hours if it was required.

"Nope, it's yours."

"Wow, thanks for calling. I can hardly hear you so I will touch base with you for the details on Monday."

I debated over how to use the Mini Cooper for the next week. I decided I would contact a few used car dealers and see how much I could presell them the car for. The highest bid came in at eighteen thousand and I informed them that I would be able to hand pick the color and options; he just needed to let me know his preference. He explained that plain and simple sells the best, so I delivered him a base model Pepper White Mini Cooper and he delivered me a certified check.

Hoping to gain control of my business, I decided to pay off a personal credit card that had been haunting us for a while and then put the rest towards my tool bill. My plan worked well enough to get me back on track for a few months, which helped my customers instill more trust in me. Once the tools came in, my customers began to purchase again, which helped me climb out of the red and into the black. However, it only lasted a short while. Sometimes situations in life are out of your control leaving difficult choices. My choice came in May of 2007 when I decided to end the situation that continued to repeat itself. At that moment, I decided no matter the outcome, I needed to end my relationship with TG and begin a new venture.

Kiddos

During the six months after winning the Mini Cooper, I was battling TG trying to get my business rolling again. The last thing we needed to be discussing was having a fourth child, but Tamika had always wanted a large family where the children were close enough in age to bond and I have always been a sucker for pleasing Tamika. I knew that if we were going to try for another son, the time to try was near. Even though my business was skating on thin ice, we both liked the idea of having two boys and two girls so Tamika and I started to discuss the realities of another pregnancy.

"After the difficult time I had carrying Lillyann, I just don't know if I can take being pregnant all over again, Cliff."

"Well, if you are good with three, I am good with three. Are you sure?"

"I think so."

Tamika had always wanted five kids leaving me pretty surprised that she was happy with only three, but God has a funny sense of humor. It seems that by the time Tamika and I had finished our conversation, she was pregnant ... again! He must have been thinking four when we were thinking three.

Tamika was in denial and could not bear the truth of what a pregnancy test would reveal so every time I would mention taking one, she refused. She waited as long as she possibly could, which happened to be on a night that we had dinner at the Smiths' house.

As we pulled up to our friends' house, the possibility that Tamika was pregnant was heavy on her mind. Feeling the morning sickness and a few other pregnancy signs, Tamika really could not deny it much longer.

"Do you think they'll notice?" Tamika asked me while looking down at her belly?

"Neah, I doubt it. You look good Tamika. Just don't swim and they'll never see your little baby bump."

We gathered our three children, all the bags that we brought for a night of food and swimming and headed to the front door of our friends' house.

"Hi; come on in. We are glad you could make it. Jeff is out by the pool grilling. Feel free to head on back. I will be there in a minute." Lindsay said as we walked in.

"I love your house. Did you decorate everything yourself?" Tamika asked while setting down the deserts and drinks we had brought.

While Tamika made small talk, our two oldest children were begging to swim, so I carried them out to the pool. "Jump in, kiddos!" I said as if anything had to be said at all. The kids were already in the pool by the time "kiddos" came out of my mouth.

"Hey, Jeff, the food smells great. Is there anything I can do to help?"

"I don't think so. Everything is going pretty smooth right now. Did you guys find our place okay?"

"Yeah, man, your directions carried us right to the driveway."

Jeff owns a local business as well, which naturally drove our topic of conversation until Tamika walked out staring at me with a large grin on her face.

"Cliff, you're not going to believe this. Lindsay thinks she may be pregnant as well."

"Really?" I asked with a shocked reaction on my face. They too already had three kids of their own.

"Yes, Cliff, and she has also been in denial. Isn't that funny?"

"That really is funny, Tamika."

"Since we have both been in denial, we decided that tonight we are going to find out together."

Although Lindsey was planning on taking the test anyway, it gave Tamika the courage to finally learn the truth. To no one's surprise, both tests came back positive and later on we learned there was only a two week difference in the due dates. The night carried on with laughter and talk about the secret both families had in common.

Tamika and I left the Smiths' house around ten and were happy the kids had worn themselves out swimming. They were all asleep when we pulled in our drive. I made my usual three trips to the car to unload each child one by one carrying each of them up the stairs to tuck them in bed. By the time I was normally done with this chore, I was tired myself. But that night Tamika and I sat out on the front porch rocking in our chairs talking about the future and how our family was about to grow. In a nervous kind of manner, Tamika spoke first saying, "I hope this pregnancy is easier on me than the last one."

"Me too, Tamika … Me too." Following my reply was silence. The remainder of our conversation mostly consisted of the noises from the night.

The following week Tamika had an appointment with her doctor. Tamika was shocked to learn that by the time her pregnancy was confirmed by the doctor, she was beyond the first trimester. Actually, this turned out to be a blessing for her. The first trimester was notorious for being hard on her. She came to the conclusion that since the first trimester yielded very little morning sickness, the remaining two should be a breeze. She was right; it should have been a breeze, but decisions I made with my business turned into something far worse than any pregnancy had thrown at her before.

Nowhere to Go

ꞁꞁ

In June of 2007, we owned a beautiful house and brand new Tahoe. We had stable jobs, two labs, three healthy children and another child on the way. We were living a very good life, but I was not happy with TG, and the thirty-five thousand dollar unexpected hit to my tool bill followed by seventy-five hundred dollars' worth of non-returnable leather jackets delivered in July was enough for me to end the contract. I had decided that it was time for a career change, but Tamika had another change she was focused on.

"Cliff, we need to talk about you getting fixed."

"Huh?! I'm sorry I did not hear you clearly. I thought you said that I needed to get fixed. Could you repeat what you really said please?"

"I'm serious, Cliff! We are good with four kids, and I think it is a good idea if you have a vasectomy before I deliver."

"Now, Tamika, you know that I will wind up being one of those guys that end up with a lifelong story of how things swelled and he walked around for a month like a cowboy who had ridden too many oversized horses. You don't want that to happen to me. Do you?"

"You better watch what you say, Cliff. You do know you can speak life into your words."

I joked around with her about the nightmarish tales told by men all the way up until the day of my surgery. Several days after the surgery, I wished I would have just kept my mouth shut and said yes ma'am from the start.

In mid-July, I had completed my inventory check-out, which according to my Zone Manager, should have zeroed out my balance due. The following week, I drove to Tallahassee, FL and purchased a very old tool truck to begin a new business as an independent tool dealer. This plan was everything opposite of Tool Group. My goal was to keep overhead low, maintain plenty of inventory full of quality tools with great warranties along with supporting the family I loved. However, not even one month into my new business, I received an official letter from the TG credit department stating that I owed one hundred and ten thousand dollars. The worst part was the balance must be paid by December or they would write it off, drastically reducing my credit score. I was livid and scared.

"They told me that I would check out okay!" I told my wife who was now in tears.

"What's going to happen, Cliff?"

"I don't know, Tamika. I just don't see how they can do this and get away with it." Feeling defeated, I looked around at the house that I loved so much and decided that we needed to sell it before it was too late.

Months went by and our house still hadn't sold. I tried to pay what I could on the tool bill, but came to a point where the mortgage fell behind, and I had to make difficult decisions. We were running very tight on money and were a couple of months past due when an offer finally came in November. With foreclosure knocking at our door, we did everything we could to speed the closing up. But roadblocks kept preventing us from scheduling the date, leaving us in fear of running out of time. If closing was delayed until December, it would not be ours to sell.

Finally, in mid-November we were able to close, and we were going to avoid foreclosure.

Financial stress can drive a wedge between two people in love. It is a tool the Enemy uses daily to keep great people from realizing their potential. God dwells in unity, and when a couple is at odds with one another, the unity is broken. Tamika regretted the decisions I had made, and I felt likewise. It is so clear to me now when I look back at the gates that I had chosen. Not a single one of them were chosen with the help of God. I was in control and didn't need His help. I really didn't even grasp the idea that I needed to consult with Him. But I do now.

When we put our house up for sale, Tamika and I fought like cats and dogs. We decided the only way to end our fighting was to find mutual ground. I proposed the idea of moving to Florence to Tamika and she agreed that it was something she would like to do. So we talked about how this would take place. Since she was still teaching and I was in transition, together we decided the best option for us was for me to begin my new business in Florence.

I parked my old beat up tool truck at Tamika's parents' house and commuted by car an hour and a half twice per day. Her mom would watch Lillyann for us during the week while Tamika and I would work. In effort to cut down on her having to travel we worked out a commuting schedule. On Monday, I would bring Lillyann with me to Florence and she would stay with Tamika's mom until I was done working for the day. At this point, Tamika's mom, Lillyann and I commuted back to Cullman. The same was done on Friday. It was not easy and took a toll on everyone. But sometimes in life you just roll up your sleeves and get it done.

What was not getting done was finding a new place to live once we had a contract on our house. I began scrambling around trying to find a place for us to live. But when you have no money in the bank, it makes it rather hard. We still had a little time left before our deadline to be out of the house and the buyers were doing all they could to help us transition. However, the stress was building a wall between us, and our marriage was beginning to take a turn for the worse.

The arguments became more and more frequent with each one becoming more intense than the last. Tamika was pregnant and I would try to keep calm, but this was all on me and I knew it. Everything was my fault, and I felt the heavy burden on my shoulders. The guilt I carried weighed a ton and the stress from the finances had my head in a vise that someone would not stop turning. Tamika came outside to the barn where I usually went to get away from life. My carpentry tools were kept out there and I would relieve stress by building things. But when she opened the door questioning me over where we were going to live, all the stress piled on again.

"I know that we are now two days before closing on the house and I have no idea where we are moving, Tamika. I don't need you yelling at me anymore! I also know that this is my fault, so just leave me alone so I can try and figure out what to do!"

My vasectomy surgery was scheduled for the next day and I was at a loss on what to do. I had convinced myself that I could no longer make a correct decision. *I used to be a person who was in control and knew what to do. What happened to that person?* I wondered.

Later that night, I received a call from my aunt. She was calling to check in on us and wanted to know what we had decided regarding our next home.

"I honestly don't know. I have nowhere to take my family when we move out."

"Do you have any money, Cliff?"

"That's just it, I have tried to do what's right and pay TG the best I could, but it drained us."

"Do you think you could come up with enough for rent at grandma and granddads?"

"For December, yes, I probably could."

"Let me make some calls and see if it's an option. I will call you back in a minute."

"Okay, thank you."

My grandparents' house would have been perfect for us and I thought for sure it would work out. So when my phone rang again, I smiled anticipating being able to tell Tamika that we would have a place to take our kids.

"Hello."

"Cliff … I'm sorry, but the house is just not ready yet."

"Not ready? What do you mean, not ready. What needs to be done?"

"Well, there are items throughout the house with labels on them showing who gets what so all of us can walk through and easily grab what belongs to us and then whatever is left over will be divided up in some sort of fashion."

"What? Everyone is putting that above helping out my family? Are you kidding me?"

"I'm sorry, Cliff. I know this upsets you."

Upset was an understatement. I had so much rage I literally thought I was going to blow up. Trying to keep from yelling, I decided to offer a solution to the issue.

"Here's what I will do. I will walk in with a camera, take a picture of each stack as it sits now and pack up each stack in a very nice and orderly way so nothing is ruined. I will place the items into a box wrapping all breakables and will then lay the picture on the top before closing it up and sealing it with packaging tape. Then, each box will be taken to the basement or wherever they desire for storage. When the day comes for everyone to get together and go through all the items, I by myself, will unload everything as it was in the picture. It will be as if no one ever touched a single thing. I don't see any reason why that will not work. My family needs a place to live." I was desperate … knowing that this was my only hope of having a place to take my family.

"I understand. Let me see what I can do, Cliff. I will call you back."

My rage turned to tears when I hung up the phone. I felt as if my family let me down. If they could not do this for me, then, I never wanted to talk to them again. When the phone rang, I was emotionally unstable as rage and tears would teeter back and forth.

"Cliff … I am truly sorry, but it is not going to work out."

Blood and anger rushed from my feet to my throat, and I let it all out. "I want you to tell all of them to lose my phone number. In fact, they can just take my name off the family phone list. Family is supposed to be there to help one another when someone is down. As far as I'm concerned, we are no longer a part of this greedy family."

I hung up the phone and started back to throw it against the barn wall, but I had already caused enough damage to last a lifetime and decided to hold onto the urge to shatter the item that delivered the news that shattered my last hope. I was furious, and at the time I meant every word I had said.

It was years before I spoke to any of the ones who played a part in that decision. When it came time to divide up all the items in the house, I only wanted one thing. It was the wooden cane that Grandaddy used when he and I would walk out together to count his cattle. The cane is priceless to me. It hangs today making up one part of an X pattern along with my Pappa's cane he used before he was bed bound. His cane makes up the second part of the X.

I paced around the yard, trying to stay out of Tamika's sight. I didn't want her to pick up on the fact that something was wrong. I couldn't bring myself to tell her more bad news, nor did I want her to know how my family had just let me down. I felt like I had just been kicked while I was down by the ones that were supposed to help me up, and I was crushed. I was done with them, but my aunt was not done with me.

She called me back; I ignored the call. Once again, she tried; once again, it was ignored. By this time Tamika had seen me and was trying to calm me down.

"Cliff, she's your aunt. You need to answer the phone. If it rings again, answer it. If it doesn't, you need to call her."

My aunt was persistent and when the phone rang again, I decided to answer the call without saying hello.

"Cliff, don't hang up on me, I have some news."

"I'm listening."

"Your uncle and I want you to move into our house. There will not be any rent charged. You will only be responsible for the utilities, cable and water."

I removed the phone from my ear and dropped my hand that carried the phone by my hip and walked away crying. I was a prideful man; I didn't show emotions and tried to hide it all from Tamika. However, a Kairos moment had just happened. God was working that day, and His love overcame my pride as I leaned on the fence weeping while in awe of the love He just displayed.

To this day, I'm not sure if my aunt and uncle truly understand what they did for my family. To put it simply, they kept our family together. After pulling myself together, I got back on the phone. "Thank you" was all I could get out of my mouth. I hung up the phone and wept some more. Later on that night, after settling down, I called my aunt to go through the details and really tell her how much I appreciated what they were doing for us.

It took me a long time to calm down, and I stayed up thinking about how my life managed to turn out the way it had. I thought about what I was doing right and what I was doing wrong. The only thing I could think of was the lack of God in my life.

I went from staring at nothing on the wall to looking down at the bottle in my hand. *Bud Light* the label read. *Why do I still drink this stuff? It doesn't help my pain … never really has. I really don't even care for the taste anymore.* I took another drink confirming the nasty taste. *Beer has never tasted good lukewarm though.* I tossed the almost empty bottle into the trash and walked to the fridge to grab a cold one. Twisting off the top I thought how a fresh cold one should taste better and took a large drink thinking that maybe if I guzzled it faster the taste I used to enjoy would come back, but it didn't. *Why don't I enjoy beer like I used to?* I decided give up on finding the flavor it once had and walked to the sink to empty the half full bottle down the drain.

As I walked into the bathroom to prepare for bed, two life-altering thoughts came to mind. *God must be working on me ... oh man, tomorrow the doctor will be working on me.*

The Power of Words

When the alarm went off the next morning, I reached over and slapped it a few times trying to hit the snooze button. The pounding in my head was intensified by the sound of the alarm. Tamika was already awake and almost ready for school before the alarm rang.

"You better get up, Cliff. It's Monday. I'm about to leave for work, and you have to carry Mandolyn to preschool. My mom should be here any minute to watch Lillyann, and you have the doctor's appointment for your surgery at 9:30, remember."

"Yes, Tamika, I remember. Hey, since you're almost ready, can you take Mandolyn with you and Brannon? My head is killing me."

"Well, you shouldn't have stayed up and drank so much last night, but if you have a hangover, I don't want you to drive her anyway, so I guess I will."

"Thank you." I decided I needed to crawl out of bed and get in the shower to begin fighting off the results of last night's activities.

How many beers did I drink? I thought while in the shower. *Three, I think.; maybe four at most.* After getting out of the shower I walked into the kitchen to look in the trash so I could get an official count.

Two..? I only drank two beers and feel this bad ... something's not right. I took a few Advil's and downed two bottles of cold water to get rehydrated, which would help begin my recovery.

After an hour or so, I felt much better. Tamika's mom was now at our house to watch Lillyann, I had on loose clothing as required for my operation and was prepared to become a changed man. The drive to the doctor's office was less than ten minutes away, and I used that time to listen to some music that would help calm my nerves.

There's nothing quite like going under the knife while awake. You remember little details about the procedure and the people around you, especially the doctor. Mine was an older gentleman who had probably performed this surgery many times with success as he was much more comfortable than me. This was to be expected. There's just nothing comfortable about lying on a table exposed while a nurse is trying to give him room to operate by holding the one thing ... well ... that's probably too much detail. Anyway, the doctor was talking, laughing and waving his bloody hands all over the room as if he was telling a story on stage while entertaining a crowd. He was having a good ol' time while I was thinking how uncomfortable the entire situation was and whishing he would lay off all the drama talk and just finish the procedure.

Outside of being uncomfortable, the surgery was not that bad. There was a pull here and a tug there. I guess the most painful part were the two shots that went directly into my ... well ... once again, it's probably too much information. Anyway, the shots were painful. However, the shots were a breeze compared to what came after the surgery.

Now if you're a man and have had this surgery, your doctor probably told you to wear a jock strap for support. Not mine, his advice was to let things hang as if I had just stepped out of the shower only with loose fit jogging pants on. This was rather shocking to me as most of my friends that had offered advice told me to purchase a good jock strap. But he was my doc and by his age he must have performed this simple procedure hundreds of times, so I trusted him and walked slowly with a slight bow in my legs, out of his office and made my journey to the place that soon was to not be my home.

A few days before Thanksgiving, I should have been back to normal. Most guys go back to work the second or third day and are back to normal by the fifth day of recovery, but not me. I had spoken life into my biggest fear and I could not believe it! This was really happening; I was really going to be one of them!

I thought back to the days when Tamika warned me about bringing life to what I was speaking and just shook my head. It had been a week since the procedure, and I hurt worse now than ever before. I called the doctor and told them something must have gone wrong. After giving them my symptoms, they scheduled me an appointment for that morning, and I made the trip back to his office.

Walking out of surgery bow legged and slow was embarrassing enough, but having to walk back in the same way was a whole other kind of embarrassment. I could not fit into jeans anymore, and the nearest parking space was at least 75 yards from the door. The journey ahead of me was going to be long and painful but had to be made. I mustered up some courage and swallowed some pride as I took the first few small steps of many that would eventually take me to his office door. So here I go, inching, and I mean inching, my way to the hospital doors in jogging pants without any underwear on. It was bad. I did not want to make eye contact with anyone, so I kept my head down and focused on just making it to the office without falling down.

When I arrived, the receptionist asked what I was there for. I informed her that I had major swelling and pain from a vasectomy performed a week ago. Still looking down while I said the words hoping no one would hear me. She marked me down and informed me that they would be calling my name shortly. I found my way to a chair and attempted to sit down which lately had become more challenging than I could have ever imagined.

Now, I am laid back and can make light of most circumstances just to ease the tension, but this was different. I was terrified and I just sat there wondering why everything that was happening was turning out the way it was. *What was I doing wrong? Why was everything around me falling apart? How can I fix things?*

My name was finally called, and the nice nurse looked over at me trying to stand up and called my name again. I looked at her and said, "You're going to have to give me a few minutes. I am a little slow today." Once we were in the room, I had to tell her why I was there, and she said, "Oh ... I'm sorry you have to go through this. The doctor will be with you in a moment." I just gave her a slight smile and thanked her.

The doctor was glancing at my charts when he walked in and said, "So, you're having a little problem?"

I let out a little laugh and said, "Well, little might not be the correct word." He asked me to drop my pants so he could to a look. Normally, I would have had them off in a flash, but this time I had to ease them down slowly stretching the front out to ensure there was not any contact. The words my doctor spoke next were priceless.

"Oh, my word, I am so sorry!"

I could not resist making a sarcastic remark before I left. "Doc, did you not wash your hands?" To this, he found no humor at all, but I felt better.

I was diagnosed with staph infection and was unable to lift anything until the swelling went down. Tamika was eight months pregnant, and we had to be out of our house by December ninth. We needed to come up with a plan fast and decided to take advantage of the Thanksgiving weekend that brought many of our friends to town. I made a few calls to the ones I knew I could count on, and it didn't take long before the word got out. We had a lot of people come to our house to help pack up and move everything. Some we knew, and some we didn't know. Regardless, they were there to move our things while we were forced to sit and watch.

At the time that my aunt offered her house to us, she and my uncle were living with her father-in-law to help him during the final months of his life. Not expecting to stay there long they had pretty much left their house as if they would be home any day. With no room for our belongings, we rented out three large storage rooms and moved all of our furniture and all the clothes we did not anticipate wearing there until we made the move to Florence.

With less than one month before our fourth child was born, I was still barely able to walk, could not lift anything over five pounds and Tamika was in the same condition. We had just moved out of what we thought at the time was our dream home, we were broke, my credit was about to be ruined and I was beginning to think that I may have an infection that antibiotics could not cure.

From the week of Thanksgiving to one week from Christmas, my life consisted of four different antibiotics, soaking in hot baths, sitting in a recliner on a hot pad, taking a lot of pain pills and walking like a cowboy that had ridden to many oversized horses. This was all done while my mother-in-law stayed with us during the week to help with the kids. I'm not sure what was more embarrassing, having to walk from the parking lot to the doctor office every week or my mother-in-law asking if I needed a hot bath. I can look back and laugh now, but during the time I was living it, I wasn't sure if I was going to survive.

Finally, at the beginning of the fourth week of misery, the doctor found an antibiotic that worked. The pain, along with the swelling, began to decrease rapidly and I was happy to be back to my normal self. Our focus turned from me to the birth of our fourth child, but not before another financial blow hit us square on the chin.

It was my first day back on the road since I had the surgery, and I was on my way to the first stop of the day. The tool truck I used for my new business was really old, and I knew there would be expenses along the way, but the timing of this one could not have come at a worse moment. While climbing a steep hill, the truck began to lose power, leading to a stall on the side of the road. It would crank, but wouldn't start leaving me to call a heavy duty wrecker service.

After having it towed into a shop I could trust to not steal anything while working on it, I waited on the diagnosis along with the quote, which came in at the amount of two thousand dollars. My daughter was scheduled to be born at the end of the week and Christmas came four days later. We had not had the chance to shop for any of the kids' Christmas gifts, and now my business was on hold until I could get the money to repair the truck. I needed something to change; however, my past of choosing incorrect gates was about to hinder my family for years to come.

In January 2008, I received my second official letter from TG Credit. Anticipating the news it had brought my hands shook while I tried to open it. I expected the letter to inform me they had written off the debt I owed, but I still couldn't bear to read it. I sat it down on the table and walked away, taking a glance back before leaving the room. The letter contained the reality of what I knew would create a struggle that a lot of people never overcome. I tried to ignore it, but the curiosity in me stirred. When I finally mustered up the courage to begin reading, my eyes followed each word carefully as the document began to unravel what I thought was to be the future of my family.

My heart sank as I read the words that told me the balance due had now become officially written off and would be reported as such on my credit. At that time, I thought they had ruined me as my credit score went from a 720 to 450, and I was devastated. However, God's plan was never for me to be in ruins. In Jeremiah 29:11, He tells us that His plan is full of hope and a future. The plan He had for me was not behind any of the gates I had chosen in the past. He had always been there with me, waiting for me to call on Him so He could take me back to the gate that lead to His plan. All I had to do was believe and listen for His voice. But, I was too busy trying to control my life and handle things on my own.

Our Fourth Child

♪

By the time our fourth child was born, you would think the hospital would just name a room on the maternity floor after Tamika. When we arrived, we checked our bags and handed the nurse our frequent flyer hospital card. Tamika, of course, being the expert on delivering babies knew the routine. So when the doctor walked in and asked if there was any need for her to stay, we all laughed.

"Being the pro you are, Tamika, I am confident you can handle this on your own," the doctor added.

"I don't think I want to do that. I'd rather you just stay."

"Well, I guess I will hang around to watch an old pro."

The contractions began around 9:00 a.m. and by 10:45, Tamika was ready to push. Our fourth child was delivered fifteen minutes later, and the doctor once again bragged on my wife.

"I hope you guys have more babies. I believe it was your calling. Besides, we need more people like you in this world."

"Ha! Too Late!" I said as she reminded me how sore I still was about the results of my surgery.

"You spoke life into that and brought it on yourself, you know." Tamika may have just delivered a baby, but she was still quick to set me straight.

I was a little nervous about how our fourth child would look. After having three gorgeous children, I was afraid the streak would end. But when I was able to get a good look at her, I knew she was just as beautiful as the rest. Everyone in the room commented on her long eyelashes. They would stop and take a double look, making some comment like, *she has the longest eyelashes. They are absolutely beautiful.* Then, some would turn to look at me and say, *you better get ready dad.*

It disturbed Tamika a lot that we did not have a place of our own for our daughter to come home to and I was disappointed too. After all, I felt as if it were my fault that we were in the position we were in. However, the day we were released from the hospital was Christmas Eve, and we made plans to have Christmas at my parents' house the next morning. It was not the same as being in our own home; however, we were blessed to have a roof over our heads and a family that loved us enough to take us in.

I wish I could say that overall life was easy during that time, but it wasn't. As you are aware, life is hard for most of us. I had to keep myself in check and knew that even though we had it bad, there's always someone else who has it worse. Some things had already taken a turn for the greater good, and for that Tamika thanked God, especially for the blessing He had just delivered to us, Melody Joy Powell.

It wasn't long until Tamika began to notice how Melody would pause when music was playing. We were both amazed at how she had already acquired a love for music. It was a love that is still being carried out today. Today, we are still captivated by the way she runs around our house, singing her songs while lighting up the room with her beautiful smile and vivacious personality. We are certain that we could not have picked a better name for our fourth child as she is truly a joyful melody to have around.

Trust

From the day Melody was born until Tamika finished up her last workday at school, life was hard. I treated Tamika like dirt and she did the same back to me. Both of us were in need of sympathy, but neither of us wanted to sympathize with the other. It was all about *"the me."*

The financial nightmare we were living had me seeking a better way, and I had become closer with God but not close enough to hear His voice or understand how He would speak to me. Not until the night that I heard Him for the first time.

Although having a place to live was a blessing, life was still extremely hard on our family while we lived in my aunt's house. Our fighting increased weekly during the time a made the daily commute from Cullman to Florence, which increased the gap between us. The hours on the road left me time to reflect on life. I thought about how I used to be in control of everything and how life seemed so wonderful. The Enemy would use that time to tell me what a sorry person I had become. How Tamika would be better off without me and I started to fall into a state of despair while convincing myself that I was no good and had ruined my family. I was not sure of our future and wasn't really sure about my life. I tried to tell myself to hang in there, but life kept beating me down.

One night Tamika and I got into a huge fight. It was one of those he said/she said stupid stuff fights that went too far and led to one of the lowest moments of my life. That night, I turned my back on my family and packed up my clothes, left her sitting on the bed crying as she tried to calm Melody's tears too.

I was stubborn at first. I drove further and further away while telling myself to not give in. *Make her call you.* But the phone never rang. I wasn't sure where I was going and just drove around until I was halfway to Florence and decided to keep moving on since I had to be there in the morning anyway. The 100 mile trip gave me plenty of time to reflect on my life. It was around 1:00 a.m. when I left Tamika and I had been on the road for at least two hours. I knew I needed to get some rest so I tried to get a room at a hotel room in Muscle Shoals but my debit card declined. *I can't even afford a cheap hotel room. I'm living in a place rent free, behind on paying my aunt for the utilities bill and have just left my family like a sorry husband and father. They would be better off if I were not even alive. I have insurance that will give them a new start. They would be better off without me.*

But God intervened. I'm not sure what would have happened that night had I not heard God's whispers. He was telling me that everything was going to be okay and to not worry. He gave me a feeling of love and hope. I sat in my car and wept until I was able to calm myself to drive on to her mom and dad's house to sleep away the rest of the night.

When I woke up that next morning, I was determined to change and called Tamika to apologize. I told her that I did not want to argue anymore and I hoped she would forgive me, which she did. I wish I could say that was the end of the Enemy interfering with our life, but I had hurt Tamika and we still battled each other until I earned back the trust I had lost.

———◆———

Unfortunately, most of the things I have learned have come from making mistakes and looking back on how to correct my incorrect decisions. It took me years to gain Tamika's trust after losing it. Most marriages would not survive what we had been through. However, they can survive if both wife and husband are willing to work at it. Trust is very important and to me, one of the most critical components to living a healthy marriage. I have learned when a wife loses trust in her husband; it takes a long time for him to earn it back. A lot of men take trust for granted not realizing how much it affects their spouse. If you're a husband, one of the greatest things you can do for your marriage is to meet the need of trust for your wife. She needs to know that she can count on you to be there when she needs you. She needs to know that she can count on you to support her and not tear her down. What she does not need is to be wondering why you're not home or what kind of shape you'll be in when you get home. She needs to feel at peace while you're away and at peace while you are at home. Be trustworthy to her, meet that need and watch your marriage strengthen.

Florence

ℐℐ

When June finally rolled around, we packed up our belongings from my aunt's house and moved them into Tamika's mom and dad's house in Florence. The move to Florence brought peace to our marriage. Tamika was happy to be with her family, and our kids really enjoyed being close to the Tennessee River where we would swim and camp. When I would get home from work, I would take the kids fishing at the pond in her dad's pasture followed by long walks with Tamika. We started to envision building a home just up the hill from the pond which restored hope for our marriage.

Although it was difficult living with nine people in the three bedroom house, life was much better for us and everyone was happy except a little boy named Brannon. The thought of starting a new school was unsettling to him. But he was willing to try, so Tamika set out for an interview at one of the elementary schools.

They were looking to hire a third grade teacher and fell in love with Tamika. She was hired on in July by the principal, but it was not official until later that month when the School Board met. Tamika was excited about moving to Florence and starting her new job. We would go to her classroom and work on cleaning it out to get ready for the new year just like we had done many times before. I was busy during the day selling tools and the school did not allow anyone in the building at night, meaning teachers did not have a key. This left Tamika having to do a lot of the work herself while I was not there.

It was mid-July and the Cullman City Schools had an upcoming board meeting in three days that would officially terminate Tamika as an employee. I am sure they had been interviewing for her position since she was already in Florence and rightfully so. The only thing Tamika really had left to do there was go in and gather up her personal belongings, which we had planned on doing over the upcoming weekend.

The next day, Tamika started working on her new room, but throughout the day, things kept coming up that left her wondering if moving to Florence was what we were supposed to do. When I got home that evening, Tamika told me everything that happened. I thought about it a long time. I even said a prayer and came to the conclusion that it was not meant for us to move to Florence. I took Tamika out by the fish pond, and we sat down on a swing that rested on the back porch.

"Tamika, I love you and I want you to be happy. If that happiness is here in Florence, then, I'm behind you 100%. However, I think God may be trying to tell you something."

"What do I do? The board is meeting in two days to make my resignation official."

"You call your principal and explain to him what happened. He will welcome you back with open arms; I am sure of it."

Tamika followed through with my advice, and we moved back to Cullman.

I believe we were obedient, and God was watching because He started to open the window and began pouring out blessings upon our family. However, I did not realize it at the time, and I kept trying to close that window. But Tamika was faithful.

Transitions

After Tamika decided to not take the job at Starling, the Lord answered my prayer. I don't really recall exactly how it came to be, but I was hired by a company selling automotive fasteners. I knew this was a temporary job that would help me transition from business owner to employee – for now, I'd let others have the headache of chasing the American dream. I expected there to be some similarities since it was an outside sales position. The freedom of keeping my own schedule is something I enjoyed and was glad to maintain. However, after a few paychecks, reality set in. I knew going in that the job was 100% commission without reimbursements on expenses, but what I did not know was how poorly the commission plan was designed. To say it was a decent job would be a lie as there were weeks I spent more on expenses than I had gained in income. I felt like I owned my own business all over again only without the headache of stocking inventory. Within two months of being with the company, I knew it was once again time to pray for a change.

While I was praying for a new opportunity, Tamika was praying for us to find a place to live that would have enough room for our family. We both had made many mistakes in the past and we knew that we must now choose the right gate, but how do you know it is the right one? I have learned to look for signs from God - clues, if you will. The most obvious signs are sometimes the things that just don't make sense, which usually means that God is involved.

One day, while Tamika was visiting my mom, she picked up the local paper to begin her search for a place to rent. The first listing she came to sounded familiar, and she wanted to check it out.

"Susan, I think I know where this house is. Do you want to ride over with me to take a look?"

"Sure, let me grab my purse and I will drive," my mom said while walking out of the room.

Tamika could not believe it. It was one of her top three favorite homes in Cullman. When I came home from work that day, Tamika was waiting with some exciting news.

"Cliff, I found us a house to look at. I have already called the landlord and she will be meeting us there at five thirty. Are you ready to go now?"

"What time is it now?"

"5:20"

"I guess so then."

Tamika told me it was the perfect place for us, but would not tell me where it was until we got there. She knew me too well and knew that I would come up with every negative reason on why we shouldn't be moving into an older home before even giving it a chance and she was right. When we pulled up to the house, I realized that it was one of her top three and glanced over at the girl who was grinning from ear to ear.

"Ok. Tamika, you know we can't afford a place like this.

"Cliff, the rent isn't that bad. I still have my job and your mom loves this house and wants us to be in it. She is willing to help us if we ever need it.

"Really?"

"Yes, Cliff. Let's go inside and check it out."

I did not have to walk in as my mind was already made up. With as much pain as I had put Tamika through in the past year there was not anything keeping me from moving our family into this house. However, I could not let her know that, so we opened the door to our future home.

"Okay, we love it. Is there any way we can purchase it in the future?" I asked the landlord as she finished showing us the house.

I wanted to begin laying out the plan to make this our permanent residence. I knew that if we had to one day move out, it would crush Tamika all over again.

The landlord replied, "I would imagine so at some point in time."

"Is it possible that we could apply the money we spend on rent as a down payment to the purchase?"

"If everything works out, and you are good renters, as I think you will be, I am willing to do that."

"Okay, then. We have a deal. Just get us some legal documents to sign, and we will get you the money you need."

For the first time in a long time, Tamika was happy and I was hopeful for our marriage.

Chicago

The day after we moved into our house, I had to leave for a week of training in Chicago for my new job. I remember thinking how uncomfortable I was going to be due to the fact that I would be sharing a room with another man that I had never met. I dreaded the trip, but I had learned that God uses circumstances such as these to plant seeds in our lives. When I opened the door to the hotel, Lee was already there. He was a middle aged man from Mississippi who enjoyed talking and reading the Bible. He was very entertaining and had a personality that almost mirrored mine. It only took a night of conversation before I trusted him enough to begin pouring my heart out to him. Throughout the next few nights, I learned how strong he was in Christ and how he too had fought some of the battles I was facing. I talked to him about how my marriage had almost fallen apart, how I put us in a situation that forced us to sell our house, the vasectomy experience and Florence. "Do you believe in Jesus? Lee asked me while looking me right in the eyes.

"Sure, I was baptized at age eight," I quickly replied as if trying to make for certain he believed me.

"Good. Are you walking daily with Him to the point that you have a relationship with Him? Do you call on Him daily for your strength?"

"Honestly, I have never really thought about it. But, no ... I guess I don't."

"Cliff, I challenge you to dig deeper and walk with Jesus daily. Learn to call on him through prayer. Learn to hear His voice when He speaks to you in His soft whisper. It is not going to be obvious, and you have to be constantly looking for Him. You may not always find Him, but He is there."

After Lee completed his sentence, he asked if he could pray for me, Tamika and our marriage. I was humbled that he cared about our marriage and knew that I had found a new friend. He was a friend that would help sharpen me over the next three years.

Fair Parade

♪♪

Tamika and I had been in our new home for over a month when the fair came to town. Cullman always kicks off fair week with a parade that is a must-see for all kids. People line up along the edge of both northbound and southbound lanes on Hwy 31. The mile long path carved in the middle of downtown Cullman brings thousands of community residents out to cheer on the local bands, thank the local responders, gaze at all the horses and buggies, smile and wave at the fair pageant representatives and catch candy from them all.

The parade of 2008 was different than years past. There was a new float that had never been seen in our small town parade. Actually … two new floats that carried around thirty people who passed out cold water and candy to the other twenty-five or so walking alongside. The walkers, as I called them, would then walk over to the crowd and pass the water and candy out to the spectators.

The sounds of sirens passing by began to be drowned out by something that to me sounded like a mix between alternative and rock music. So I was shocked to learn that it was Christian. I had never listened to Christian rock music in my life, and I didn't know that we had a church in town that played it. My seven year old son looked at me and said, "I want to go to that church!"

Noticing how everyone had smiles on their faces, I thought the same thing.

The next morning, I intentionally sat in the recliner reading the Sunday paper trying to look as if I didn't know what time it was. When Tamika came in and asked if I was going to church, I told her not unless we tried Daystar. "What about the church we have been attending? I feel obligated to go to it."

"I don't; I get more out of watching Joel Osteen on TV than I get out of the preaching there. Tamika, I just want to try a new church."

"Cliff, just please get ready. I don't want to be walking in late again; it's embarrassing and you know that everyone notices."

I could tell that Tamika was getting really upset, and I did not want to have a knock down drag out over going to church. So, I got up to change my clothes. The argument continued from the time I got out of the chair until we pulled up to our church.

"I'm not going in this late."

"You're kidding me right?"

"No, Cliff. I'm not kidding we are fifteen minutes late. Let's just go back home."

A smile came across my face as I pulled out of our old church parking lot because I knew I was driving to Daystar.

"Where are you going?"

"I'm going to Daystar." I looked back in the mirror, and my son had a grin on his face that confirmed my decision.

"You know we are going to be even later there."

"Yes, Tamika, I know. But I have a feeling that they don't care. Besides, the church is so large that we can probably sneak in and sneak out without anyone really knowing."

When we pulled up to the campus, we were amazed at the amount of people directing our way to a parking space. It was something that you would see at a concert or large event. "This must be one large church, Tamika. They have so many people they have to direct traffic."

After parking the car, a very nice gentleman pulled up on a golf cart and asked if we would like a ride to the front doors.

"Yes!" the kids all said at once.

Walking in the front doors we were greeted with smiling faces, handshakes and just about everyone stopped us to complement our children. We felt the love of Christ from the moment our car hit the parking lot.

Once inside the building, I was impressed with the industrial appearance that catered to a man's taste. My kids could not get over the themed appearance of KPC (Kids Power Company). When we checked them in, we were educated on how the beeper worked in case our children needed our attention. After our kids were inside KPC, Tamika and I walked over to the coffee shop to get us a cup before we entered the auditorium.

Immediately after worship, our beeper notified us that one of our children needed us. It was our youngest daughter Melody, she would not calm down. I told Tamika that I would check on her and never made it back in to hear the sermon. While Melody and I sat in the lobby and played, Tamika cried her eyes out during the message. She had never heard preaching like what she heard that day and was completely moved by the Holy Spirit.

After service, a regular member came up to us and asked how we enjoyed the pastor's sermon.

"I loved it." Tamika told them while wiping away the massacre that had smeared from crying.

"Just wait until you hear the lead pastor."

"What?" Tamika asked. "You mean he is not the lead pastor?"

"No, the lead pastor is Jerry Lawson. He is out of town this weekend, but will be back for next weekend. You should come back to hear him. He has a different approach and is wonderful also."

Tamika was now sold on Daystar and I was too, but how did our kids like it, we wondered. From the reactions they gave us when we picked them up from KPC, it appeared that they loved it. However, we really did not know how much they loved it until the following Sunday.

The work week passed by fairly quickly, and it was Sunday morning again. Tamika and I were debating on which church to attend that day. She, once again, had a guilty feeling about not going to our old church, and I was trying to be more sensitive this time. Just about the time we were getting out of bed to get ready, our two oldest kids came to our bedroom door dressed for church!

"We are ready to go to Daystar; get up and get dressed!" Tamika and I could not believe our eyes and felt very proud.

She turned to me and said, "It looks like we're going to Daystar."

Trapped by the Enemy

My family dove in head first, drowning ourselves with Daystar and Jesus. We could not get enough and attended the Sunday morning, Sunday evening and Wednesday evening services every week. Even when we had a lot going on at home and I did not want to attend the Sunday evening service, Tamika was quick to point out, "Cliff, it's the Believers Service, and if we are Believers then we must attend."

Her words worked on me every time. I would give in saying, "You're right Tamika. I guess I need to stop what I'm doing and go get ready."

Every time we would attend the Believers Service I would walk a little bit closer with our Lord. I never regretted putting everything aside on Sunday afternoon to attend another church service. We were growing in our walk with Christ, and it was good for us - especially the night we were prayed over by Roger.

It was a worship experience that had everyone who attended raising their arms in praise. I had chills throughout my body and was unsure if it was just cold in the room or if the Holy Ghost really was present. At the time, I was young in my walk with Christ and still hanging onto my worldly ways of analyzing everything and putting faith in little. Tamika was sold out. She began praying over everything and everybody in my house and I have to say … it freaked me out a little. But she was strong in her faith and knew what our marriage needed. It needed prayer and lots of it.

It must have been the Holy Ghost moving that night because Roger Hamm walked up to Tamika and me asking if he could pray over us. "I don't know why, but the Holy Spirit has moved me to speak life over your family." Tamika was tearing up as we bowed our heads. The words Roger spoke were powerful. Words like: *Your family will do great things for His church* and *Your family will make a difference in the world through the struggles you face; you will have a testimony that will change lives.* At the time, I simply thanked Roger for the prayer. But Tamika was to the point of crying as she began to share with him the struggles I had been going through.

Since we started to attend Daystar, everything in our marriage would be good for a few months, and then something would happen that is hard to describe. I told Tamika one time that it was like the Enemy would grab a hold of me and would not let go. I changed for a couple of hours out of nowhere and became a person that I feared. We would get into some little argument most of the time over he said/she said stuff and my temper would erupt. There were two or three times when it was so bad that Tamika would try to hide from me - scared to death that I would hurt her.

I was a little uneasy about Tamika sharing my issues with Roger. At the time, I was still full of pride and did not like anyone to know about my weaknesses. I didn't understand that in order for a wound to heal, the wound needs to be exposed. And, I didn't want anyone knowing about the way I talked to my wife at times. I didn't want anyone to know that one night I was so angry that I walked by and punched a tall picture frame that enclosed a collage of photos of our kids breaking the glass out and cutting up my hand. I did not want anyone to know that when my wife crawled into a ball and prayed for Jesus to help me, I would yell at her and poke fun of her for praying to Him thinking He would solve everything. I did not want anyone to know that one night

I ripped pages out of my Bible and cursed Jesus. I did not want anyone to know that I was trapped by the Enemy, an Enemy that would not let me go. But she had always believed in the power of prayer and knew that Matthew 18:19 (NIV) states, "… if two of you on earth agree about anything they ask for, it will be done for them by my Father in heaven."

Roger listened closely and agreed with her in faith that my struggles would soon end, and the peace of Jesus would dwell among our family. It did not happen immediately and there were a couple more battles, but God worked on me and He used others to surround me in prayer. Looking back now, I know God used Roger to prophesy over us and there is no doubt in my mind that he did hear from the Holy Spirit that night. At the time, he didn't know how much life he was speaking into our family nor did we. But I am glad that he was a faithful servant that opened the door for us to be where we are now. I have never shared this with Roger, and he may not even remember praying over us, but I remember and I am forever grateful to him for doing so. One thing I have learned from the prayer that night is this: if your struggles are kept to yourself, how will anyone know how to be praying for you? This world we live in is spiritual, and our battles need to be fought as such. The more exposed you become, the more people can be in prayer for you. I believe the larger your army of warriors are, the more likely God will be moved to act. So find a godly man or woman who will sharpen you, and when you know that you can trust them, share.

Generational Curses

ॐ

The Enemy is sneaky and had a strong hold on me. I was a new believer and didn't know how to fight the spiritual battle I had found myself in. I was unaware of what the Bible meant in Ephesians 6:10-18 (NIV).

> "[10] Finally, to be strong in the Lord and in his mighty power. [11] Put on the full armor of God, so that you can take your stand against the devil's schemes. [12] For our struggle is not against flesh and blood, but against the rulers, against the authorities, against the powers of this dark world and against the spiritual forces of evil in the heavenly realms. [13] Therefore put on the full armor of God, so that when the day of evil comes, you may be able to stand your ground, and after you have done everything, to stand. [14] Stand firm then, with the belt of truth buckled around your waist, with the breastplate of righteousness in place, [15] and with your feet fitted with the readiness that comes from the gospel of peace. [16] In addition to all this, take up the shield of faith, with which you can extinguish all the flaming arrows of the evil one. [17] Take the helmet of salvation and the

sword of the Spirit, which is the word of God. [18]
And pray in the Spirit on all occasions with all
kinds of prayers and requests. With this in mind,
be alert and always keep on praying for all the
Lord's people."

None of this made sense to me, but, Tamika is a strong woman with a lot of faith and was prepared for the spiritual battle. When the Enemy would twist our words and manipulate our conversation, I would become a puppet on strings and begin acting like a jerk by belittling my wife. The strings were tight allowing the Enemy to manipulate my moves with ease. The devil enjoyed playing with me as he knew I was still under his control. However, Tamika stood on a rock named Jesus and would fight the Enemy with words like - *In Jesus' name I demand the devil to leave this house.*

She understood that we were in a spiritual battle and fought with prayer while I fought with alcohol. When the fight became too much for her to take, she would lock herself in a quiet place separated from me and pray while I would turn to the bottle. Knowing I was in the wrong, I sat in another room wondering what was going on with me. I knew I needed to repent, but I felt bad that I had failed Him again. What I know now is that even though I had turned away from God many times, He was always with me. I know that He was watching over me, waiting for the moment that I would call out His name so He could rescue me once again. Only this time, it would be forever.

A few weeks after Roger spoke life into us, I was captivated by the message our pastor was delivering. It was my first time to hear the two words- generational curses- used together. I wasn't sure exactly what it meant, yet the more I listened, the more I understood it was what was going on in my life.

I thought back to the time when I was in fourth grade and my dad taught me how to mix him a bourbon and diet coke. The time

I learned that my Grandmother walked into my uncle's house and emptied the beer from his fridge because my grandfather could not be tempted. I then thought about my mom's side of the family and how everyone in the family drank some sort of alcohol. I thought about the many times I drank too much and made a fool out of myself. Lastly, I thought about how I had neglected my kids many times due to a hangover and how I had been a complete jerk to my wife for so many years.

I lowered my head as tears ran down my face, and I prayed to God to help me overcome my generational curse. I decided right then and there -never again. Never again will my kids be raised around alcohol. Never again will I wake up with a hangover. Never again will I choose alcohol over my kids. Never again will this curse run in my family. Never Again!

After leaving church, I anticipated what I had to do as I drove home. When we walked in the house, the kids went upstairs to play, Tamika went to change into some more comfortable clothes, and I went to the kitchen to end the curse that was wrecking my life. *What should I do with all of this liquor?* I thought as I stood in front of the wine cabinet staring at all the bottles it held. *Should I give it back to mom and dad? No, that would not be good for them. In fact it's not good for anyone. I will just dump it down the sink. That's right, dump it out.*

Grabbing bottle number one, I hesitantly opened the cap and slowly, with almost a bit of regret, I began to pour a little bit of a half-gallon of vodka down the sink drain. The more I poured, the more I felt the love of Jesus. I went to get the second bottle, which was a half-gallon of tequila and began to dump it out. What relief I felt as it flowed out of the neck and into the drain that led to the sewer. The more bottles I emptied, the better I felt, and I knew that all of Heaven must have been rejoicing because I could feel the happiness inside of me.

When I was done, I took all the empty bottles and sat them on the street next to the trashcans that was to be picked up the next day. After setting the last one down, I counted them. *Thirty-two, wow.* Thirty-two empty bottles that once held the poison the Enemy used for generations to destroy my family. The liquor was out of my house and my new life was about to begin.

A New Identity

Shortly after emptying the bottles, I realized something else must change as well. A decision to end an addiction is a huge battle. It's a battle in which a complete life change must take place. The best way I can really describe it is an identity change. Only, the new identity was not new to God. I was going back to the person God intended me to be the entire time. It was the world that had changed my identity and I was now becoming the person I was meant to be.

This was not easy, and I had to be very honest with myself. Was I willing to complete the journey that God had for me? If so, I knew that I had to admit my weaknesses, which was hard for a man who's full of pride. I wanted to be in control of my life, but I needed to let go and allow God to take control. I knew that I had a hard time saying no to anything offered by anyone and decided to be stronger in resisting. I also knew that all temptations in my future needed to be abandoned.

A complete life change … that was my goal, and my focus was now on Jesus. I wanted to walk in the path He had paved for me. I knew that Revelations 3:16 told me that Jesus discarded any lukewarm faith, and I was finished being lukewarm. It was time for me to give my life back to the one who gave His life for me. I was on fire for God, and I was willing to follow Him no matter the cost.

The following month started off with Baptism Sunday. I told Tamika that I was going under. I had been baptized at the age of eight, but four years later turned my back on God. I hankered for the washing of my sins. The thought of stepping into the water a spiritually dirty man and coming out spiritually clean with a new start brought chills to my skin and tears to my eyes. To make it even more special, Tamika and Brannon decided they, too, would be baptized with me. This brought a special joy to my heart and made it a day I will never forget.

Daystar only baptized once a quarter during that time, and God had been working miracles and changing lives, so the line was long. Tamika, Brannon and I were part of the last third of eighty-two people to be cleansed that day. The anticipation began to rattle my nerves a little. I debated on waiting until another time until I realized the Enemy was creating doubt and fear, and I was playing right into his plan. Procrastination is a sin, and I realized if I procrastinated the Enemy would win. That was not happening, not on this particular day. I was there to humiliate the devil and stomp on his head. It was a day to rejoice, and when it came time for me to go under … tears filled my eyes.

There, in the baptistery, stood a man in his early thirties with a past full of regret weighing him down, admitting to the crowd how he had failed God, his mom, his wife and his children. I did not plan on saying anything, but felt moved by God to explain how I had chased what I thought was considered "cool" for over twenty years followed with how I was wrong. I leaned over, peering into the crowed and spoke into the microphone, "Getting drunk, chasing women and experimenting with drugs is not cool … This is cool!"

Pastor Jerry followed up with an "Amen," and asked me, "Have you received Jesus Christ as your Lord and Savior?" As soon as I said, "I do accept Jesus," he completed his statement and pulled me under. Water rushed over me slowly, transforming me from the old sinful man into a new man of purity. I could feel the burdens of my past being released, and even though the water contained filth of more than sixty dirty bodies, it felt clean and fresh as it washed over me from back to front and head to toe. When I came up, I was a new man. A man on a mission to serve God in whatever way He asked. There was only one question remaining. Could I be as faithful to Him as He had been to me?

Serve

A few weeks after Baptism Sunday, the church sermon was on serving in and outside the church. Tamika and I were not involved outside of attending every service, and I felt compelled to keep my promise that I had made with God to serve Him. At the time, our church offered seven ministry teams that were in need of volunteers. We researched all of them trying to find the perfect one for us. Tamika prayed about which team to be on, and I made my first mistake as a new man. Control was a weakness as I felt that I had it all figured out. I failed to pray and patiently wait on God to guide me like Tamika had done.

"I think we should join the Care Ministry Team." Tamika told me the Saturday night that followed the sermon on serving.

"That sounds like a great thing for you to join."

"So it's done then; we will join the Care Ministry Team tomorrow."

"I am not good with people who have problems. I don't like praying out loud with anyone. Besides you have the kind heart and care about the feelings of others when they are hurting. I'm better off serving in something technical like production or video."

"Cliff, I really feel like God is calling us to Care Ministry. We need to sign up for it tomorrow. It'll be okay and you'll get used to it." Knowing I was not going to win this battle, I submitted to her; however, I had my doubts that I would enjoy it.

The next day at church we signed up for Care Ministry. The more and more we served in Care Ministry, the more I realized how right Tamika had been. I did warm up to it and saw a lot of value in reaching out to others, especially the time when God showed up and changed a life I will never forget.

Tanya was nine months pregnant and homeless when she attended our church for the first time. There was an appointment God had arranged that day, but neither person new the time, date or reason they would meet. After the service, Tamika caught up with Tanya in the lobby asking her if she would like to have a couple of refreshments and meet the pastor. Tanya and her cousin thought it would be nice to let him know how much his sermon impacted them and decided to go with Tamika. Church members had cornered Pastor Jerry after service which kept him from arriving at his normal time. That's the way God works; His timing is always perfect. While waiting on Pastor Jerry to arrive, Tamika and I engaged in a conversation with Tanya and her cousin to help them relax.

Somewhere in the conversation, the topic of Tanya's current situation was brought up. During the middle of her story, Tanya looked up and saw my wife in tears. Silence replaced her voice that had been telling us about her drug addiction and how she was kicked out of her apartment and she too began to cry.

Softly, in a voice full of unbelief, Tanya asked Tamika, "Are you crying for me? I've never had anyone cry for me before."

Tamika and Tanya both were in tears and hugged one another beginning a transformation that amazes me to this day.

Tanya came back to Daystar the following week and to my knowledge every week after. Jesus had touched her and filled her life with blessings from complete strangers who began to pour into her life. The love of Christ transformed Tanya from a homeless, pregnant lady, who was trying to break a long time addiction to drugs, to a Christian mom who has witnessed more miracles in one year than most see in a lifetime.

Witnessing this gave me a new perspective on Care Ministry and the purpose God saw in it. Through Tanya's story, I began to see the value in what we were doing by reaching out to those who were attending for the first time, and I was beginning to warm up to serving on the team, just as Tamika had stated. However, Tamika wanted to dive in deeper. She felt led to join a team that I was not comfortable with at all. I knew it would be a challenge that would test my faith.

"Cliff, let's join the Prayer team too."

"Prayer team?"

"Yes, Cliff the prayer team, you know the altar prayer partners that come down and pray at the end of service. I think God is calling us to join the team. I really want to do this, Cliff."

Tamika was convinced that He was telling her that we needed to join the team, and for several weeks she would continue to push me to join with her. But prayer was my biggest weakness. I had never prayed out loud or in front of anyone before. The fact was I didn't know how to talk to someone who wasn't physically there. As a teenager, when my mom asked me to say the blessing I always felt ridiculous and would usually blow it off with a sarcastic, "rub a dub, dub thanks for the grub, let's eat." I could pray silently, but to speak words out loud made me feel very uncomfortable. Thankfully, there was another ministry that God called me to.

Three months after we started Care Ministry, there was an announcement made regarding free food upstairs. Maybe Tamika and I came in late and missed the reason they were handing out food that day, or maybe I was paying half attention. Whichever one, we only heard… free food. As soon as church dismissed, I gathered up my family, and we all headed to the second level of the building where lunch was to be served. Still relatively new to the church of eight hundred members, we were a little unsure of all the in's and out's. Had we known the food was for volunteers interested in helping with the youth, we probably would have chosen another place to eat. But God used a free lunch to help show Tamika and me what His plan was for our future as church volunteers.

After the youth pastor (Troy) blessed the food, I walked up to the pizza line and noticed that I was standing directly behind his wife, Kelly. Still feeling a little unsure as to exactly what was going on; I reached out and tapped her on the shoulder hoping that I would not have to speak too loudly, "Hi Kelly, Tamika and I came up here thinking the entire church was invited. What is this actually for?"

"Oh, I see. We are feeding all of the current youth workers and anyone who is interested in serving with the youth. Are you interested in working with the youth group?"

"No, I mean I didn't know … umm, I guess we misunderstood. I'm sorry; we should probably leave."

"No, you don't have to leave. Really, it's okay. Y'all can stay and eat. Don't feel bad. It's a simple mistake. Feel free to eat as much as you like."

"Okay. Thank you."

As we inched our way down the food line, I felt God come upon me and tell me I was there for Him. Taken aback about what I felt, I was encouraged to speak up once more. "Hey, Kelly, what if we decide to help out with the youth. What do we need to do?"

"Just hang out after lunch is finished and there will be a very brief meeting on how you can get involved. I'm glad to hear you may have had a change of heart."

I went back to the table and told Tamika the news about helping out with the youth. She said, "This doesn't get you out of Care Ministry you know." Of course she was kidding, and I just laughed knowing that she understood how uncomfortable Care Ministry was for me at the start. However, I was just as uncomfortable helping with the youth but felt moved by God to step out of my comfort zone and truly begin to follow Him.

For the next six months, I tried to figure out my role in the youth department and how I could use my talents to advance His

Kingdom. We all have talents inside us. Some talents are used on stage in front of a congregation, while others are used behind the scenes. My talent was in administration, so I sat back and picked apart what was going on in youth and how things could improve. While I tried to figure out how to improve the youth ministry, Troy and Kelly were trying to figure out where they were to carry out the mission God had for them.

Troy had a heart for third world countries, and Kelly was deeply rooted to Alabama. She felt strongly in her heart that their mission was here, but Troy disagreed. He begged to hear from God, looked for signs and sought after unanswered questions, but God's timing is perfect and when Taylor and Amy, two angels dressed in raggedy clothes with filthy faces, appeared in his life, he had no choice but to submit to God's plan and admit to Kelly he was wrong.

Taylor is the same age as Mandolyn, and Amy is a year older than Lillyann. Our girls had been gathering some gifts to give the girls on the day Kelly picked them up. I was unaware of the lesson on generosity Tamika had begun discussing with our girls. She talked to them about the importance of giving generously and how they could make a positive impact in lives of others. Kelly's youngest son had spent the night with Brannon on the day she picked up Taylor and Amy and stopped by our house to pick up him up. When they walked in, my girls hugged the two girls who were mere strangers and spent time showing them the items they had gathered for them. I was surprised to see they had chosen some of their favorite toys to give away. A smile of happiness came across my face as they cheerfully gave them to their new found friends. Had I not chosen the gate that ended the generational curse, I probably would have missed out on witnessing the great deed of that day.

Mandolyn and Taylor's birthdays were only a few days apart, and they decided to celebrate turning eight together. During the party, I could tell something was going on by the looks on Troy's and Kelly's faces. They had just learned the current administrator I was under stepped down from his role, which left Troy in a mess. While Troy left for church that night, Kelly stuck around to help clean and visit. She proceeded to tell us that Troy did not know what he was going to do or who he was going to get as a replacement.

Sitting there, I began to think about my job and how it kept me busy as well as kept us fed. But it was then that I realized how I needed to build my faith in the one I served and give away a little control. I prayed, seeking a word from God while listening to Kelly tell Tamika a little more about how Troy had to have a strong administrator. Spiritually, I felt good about what I was about to offer and decided to speak up. "Kelly, if Troy's interested … I could probably help him out a good bit."

"Oh, really, that would be fantastic. You are just what he would need. I think it would be a perfect fit and will mention it to him. I'm sure that he or I will let you know for sure within a few days."

I was aware of the commitment I had just made and knew that it would probably interfere with my career, but I also knew that my heart was in it for the right reasons. If I lost my job doing what I felt God called me to do, then I was just messing up His plans with that job anyway. Jeremiah 29:11 tells me that God knew His plan for me before I was in my mother's womb. As long as I was doing God's work, I felt that I was being obedient and living out what His plan was for me. I decided to put complete trust in the Lord and His plan for me … whatever it looked like.

My ministry with Troy began within the two weeks following Mandolyn and Amy's party. I poured my heart into it as if I was a full time employee. The way I viewed it, the work I was doing was not for money but for the Lord. And the Lord gave me a new life full of hope, which inspired me to share His word. I desired to make a difference and help others learn how real God is and how walking in His footsteps led to a better quality of life. It's not a life of wealth or a life where you can get what you want when you want it – it's a life of peace, a life of love and a life of hope. It's knowing that you have someone you can trust. Someone you can count on to guide you into the right decision when you can't decide which gate to choose. But I warn you … it's not easy, and it takes a lot of faith.

Proverbs 21:17 tells us that iron sharpens iron, so one person sharpens another. If I were a piece of iron when I started helping Troy, I would have been as round as an iron rod. I think Troy could see that in me as he started randomly striking me with wisdom when I least expected it. The blows were forceful, and during the first three years of working with him in youth, I was transformed from a round rod of iron into a polished sword ready to conquer any spiritual battle.

The Enemy is sneaky and will make every attempt to interrupt the plans God has for you. God gave us free will allowing us the freedom to come to Him if we choose. He is neither a dictating God nor one that forces you to serve Him. He loves you and yearns for you to draw near to Him. On the other hand, this freedom is also dangerous. Free will leaves us vulnerable to the Enemy's attack. If you are not willing to call on Jesus, the Enemy will destroy you. This is something I know very well.

In April, 2012 I was sharper than I had ever been. Fourteen months earlier, Troy had been called to serve as the campus pastor for the Daystar Church Hartselle Campus forty minutes north of us. He asked if I would be willing to be his administrator over the campus. Humbled by the fact that God would want to use me in a way that could impact many lives, I happily committed.

The first year had been a year of adjustments, and we were finally at the point that new visitors were more frequent, lives were being transformed and everyone could feel the presence of God showing up each Sunday. I felt really good spiritually about what we were doing and had more faith in God than ever before. The past four years of iron clashing with iron had made me sharp, but around the corner was the Enemy ready to try and destroy my faith forever.

The Wound that Never Healed

♪♪

Our town was coming up on the one year anniversary of an F4 tornado that ran through the middle of our city. The tornado missed my house by a few blocks sparing us from damage and injuries. My parents were not as lucky. Physically the damage from the storm didn't harm mom or dad, but the damage sustained emotionally was one of the final pieces to the puzzle of depression that eventually took dad away from us forever.

On our way home from a church meeting, Tamika and I decided to treat the kids to some yogurt since they behaved so well. Tamika and I had just sat down and were discussing the upcoming week when my phone rang. I checked to see who was calling as I didn't really want to be pulled away from the yogurt nor the conversation, but it was mom and I knew I needed to take the call.

A call from mom on Sunday is normally regarding dinner plans, but this call was one like no other. It started out with her sobbing mixed with her effort to pull it together. I knew something was terribly wrong, and I tried to calm her down enough to determine what was going on. My mind was racing with thoughts of what could be wrong.

"Mom … what's going on?" I was growing more and more concerned by the minute as she could not gain her composure. "You don't have to go into any details right now; just tell me where you are." I turned and looked at Tamika to signal her that it was time to go.

Tamika could read the look on my face and knew something bad was wrong. As I climbed into our Tahoe, she asked softly if I knew what was going on. "I don't know she's just very upset and could hardly get her words out without crying. I think it's best if you and the kids stay at the house while I check to see what's going on."

By the time I pulled out of my driveway to find mom, I could feel the lump in my throat signaling our nearly perfect day was about to come to an end. As I pulled up behind mom, I noticed my uncle standing next to her car and thought to myself how something bad must have happened. As I neared her car, I could hear my dad's slurred voice on the speaker phone throwing out one curse word after another. The mental beating he was giving mom was weighing on her heavily. I could tell that she was worn down and reaching the point of enough.

Hearing all I could take, I stepped away from her car and tried to calm myself down. I said a quick prayer and asked for wisdom from God. If anything was going to keep me from beating dad to a pulp, it was Jesus, and I needed Him worse than ever before. Mom needed Him too and I knew it. After taking all she could stand, the inevitable was finally done as she hung up on the man that had replaced the person I knew as dad. The look on mom's face told me one of two things. Either she had grown numb to his words, or my prayer for her strength was being answered. Whichever it was, she now had calmed down enough to begin walking me through the events that had led up to her leaving.

"I thought he had fallen asleep. The drinking started earlier than normal last night and continued all throughout the morning. He needed to sleep, so when I got back from church ..." Mom kinda stared off into space as if replaying the event in her mind. "I should have gone up there. None of this would have happened. I tried to be quiet. I didn't want to wake him. I guess he never was asleep. Shortly after I got home, he started yelling for me to come up stairs. Often times in the past, he has had episodes of yelling and fighting while appearing to be awake. But each time he drew a blank not being able to remember the night before. In his mind, the yelling and fighting never happened. He never believed me until one day when he noticed a dent in the refrigerator. It was placed there the night before from him hitting it with a broom."

Her story was interrupted by another call from dad. When mom answered, all we heard was more cursing and yelling. Feeling stronger, mom immediately hung up on him. "I was scared, Cliff. I knew that I might need to make a quick run for the car, so I hung my purse on the door with my keys in it. That's when I heard him coming down the steps yelling at me. His voice was full of rage and hate. He was angry and had a look in his eyes like I had never seen before. He threw up his arms and then started to push me around as I tried to calm him down. It kept getting worse … I tried to get away but he reached out and grabbed my neck. He wasn't choking me, but his fingers were digging in to hang on. I don't know how, but I was able to break free from him. When I did, I grabbed my purse and ran to the car. I wasn't sure what to do. I drove around for a while trying to decide where to go and what to do. I knew that you had a meeting today, and I didn't want to talk while the kids were in the car with you, so I decided to pull over and call your uncle for his advice."

After hearing her story, I knew it was too dangerous for her to go back home to get her clothes. I also knew, if I went by myself, dad and I would get into it. At the time, I was angry that he had hurt mom and was afraid that I would not be able to hold myself back. We decided it would be best to call the police and have them meet us at the house while she gathered her clothes.

When the police arrived, we walked them through what happened, and they followed mom to her house. On the way over, I ran a list of items through my mind that I wanted to get out of the house. Depression and alcoholism is a generational curse that has plagued his family for years and I was hoping to prevent another calamity. When I walked through the door, I went to the living room where I found dad. He was taken aback when he saw me and tried to act sober, but his slurred speech was evidence proving otherwise. I was focused on my task at hand and quickly told him that I wasn't interested in talking to him while he was drunk; I just wanted to know where all the guns and alcohol were kept. "If you walk up the stairs, there's a .357 on the table. It's loaded so be careful. The double barrel is in the basement."

"What about the liquor?"

"It's outside in the storage building behind my toolbox."

As I turned to head upstairs, his phone rang. It was his boss on the other end returning a call from dad. I continued up the steps as dad began to tear into his boss making for certain everyone in the house could hear what was going on. *He quit his job … mom's gathering her clothes … he now knows that I know everything that happened today … he's not planning on seeing tomorrow.*

⊷◆⊶

At the age of fifteen, dad took a walk on the dirt road which led from his parents' house to the small house his grandparents lived in. It was a walk that would haunt him the rest of his life. When he entered the house, no one was in the living room as normal. He meandered into the kitchen where a butcher knife laid on the floor next to a trail of blood that led to the bedroom. Nervously, the young teenager crept into the bedroom fearing what he would find. As he peaked in, he found his grandparents lying on the bed. The head of his grandmother was resting on his granddads shoulder with his granddad's head resting on her head. A pool of blood saturated the sheets on the bed and a gun was affixed into the cold hand of my great-grandfather's lifeless body. No one really knows exactly what happened that day or how the events resulted to the deaths of a couple who seemed to be happily married. But we do know the image my dad saw that day became an image he tried hard to drink away.

Mom later told me that she was afraid what happened to them would one day happen to her. As I gathered the liquor, guns and ammo … I too felt what she was talking about. Dad was clearly not in his right mind, and I did not want to be left alone in the house with him. While mom gathered her clothes and the police officer encouraged dad to not do anything stupid once we left, I carried the items I found to my car. After the first trip I remembered the .22 rifles dad owned. I went to the basement to search one last time and told myself to not forget the knife set from the kitchen that contained butcher knives and steak knives. I searched in every corner of the basement and decided to head upstairs hoping to find them in the closet. But when I reached the top of the steps, I could hear the car doors slam and realized I was about to be left alone with dad who was now stumbling back towards the house to come inside. A decision had to be made; I had four children and a wife that I loved very much. I could not afford to be in a situation that could endanger my life or his. Thinking that my brother could have the .22's, I decided to go ahead and leave while I could.

Dad must have heard the door open and asked me if I had some time to help him clean out the cab of the truck he drove for his former employer. I saw no harm in it and thought it might give him some time to sober up as well as give me some time to try and talk some sense into him. I spoke words of encouragement and shared the love of Christ with him. When we finished cleaning the truck, I asked what I should do with all the stuff. His response warned me of his intentions. "Just throw it in my pickup. Someone can clean it out when they go through it later."

"Dad, you need to think about the six grandkids that love you. You need to focus on hope and give your burdens to Jesus. Try dad, just ask Him to come into your life and try." He asked if we could go inside and talk, but I had traveled that road many times while he was under the influence. It never led to any change. I politely told him, "Not while you're drunk, dad. I can in the morning when you sober up." I kept thinking about my wife and kids at home and how I was not putting myself inside the house with it just being the two of us. "I need to go dad; Tamika is probably worried about me." I wrapped my arm around his shoulder to give him a side hug and told him I loved him for the first time in my life.

As I pulled out of his driveway I felt pretty good. I had removed all the guns, bullets and liquor. As long as my brother had the .22's, dad would have time to sober up and rest safely. *In the morning, I will check on him. Oh no, no ... shoot. I forgot the knives. Surely, he won't use a knife on himself. Surely not ...*

The drive from his house to mine was less than a five minute commute and ten minutes after I walked in, my phone rang. My brother was on the other end of the line asking me if I knew what was going on with dad. "Why do you ask?" I replied.

"He called me just a minute ago and told me he loved me. He sounded pretty drunk."

"He is ... I just left there. You may want to go see him ... then again, maybe you shouldn't. He's unpredictable right now. But I will leave it up to you. I will tell you this though; this may be the last day you will get to talk to him. I have a bad feeling he may try to kill himself."

I had to let my brother go due to another call. It was my cousin on the other line telling me that dad had called our aunt to tell her he was ending it today. "He must have been pretty convincing as she said that she believed him and someone needed to check on him right now." I told my cousin thanks for letting me know and I was calling the officers to meet me at dad's.

On my way out the door, I dialed 911 and headed out the drive. Emotions ran through my body as I cautiously ran through every red light I could. My hope was to make it there in time to keep him from doing something stupid, but when I arrived something held me back. I pulled into his drive, put my car in park and made my way to the back door until something came over me. I stopped dead in my tracks and turned back to the car and paced back and forth. Considering the chances that he had the .22 rifle I couldn't find when I gathered his guns, I thought about my family again. *I can't take a risk of dying today. I have four kids and a wife who needs me, but he wouldn't shoot me … or would he. He was very drunk and out of his mind. That's stupid, Cliff; he wouldn't shoot you. Now go in there and check on him.* Just before I reached the door, the officers pulled up. I walked over to them to let them know what was going on and asked what I needed to do. After telling me to just stay by my car, they went to the front to see if they could see him through the windows, which were out of my sight.

The adrenaline rushed through my body as I waited. My senses were on high alert trying to detect anything that would provide a clue as to what was going on. I heard a quick round of what sounded like gunshots were being fired. Reaching an emotional peak, I exploded like a volcano boiling over with emotions. I lost complete control of myself and didn't know what to do except call someone closer to Christ than me. The amount of tears pouring from my eyes combined with my inability to stop shaking hindered my ability to make out the letters on the phones keypad as I searched for Troy's name. After, multiple tries, I finally dialed Troy's number and prayed that he would answer. "They're killing him Troy; pray for my dad; they're shooting my dad!"

"What? I can't understand you, Cliff. I know you're upset, but you're going to have to calm down for a minute and tell me what's going on."

"The police are at my dad's house, and I guess they got in. He must have found his .22 because all I hear now are gunshots." The gunfire sounds stopped, and I noticed one of the officers walking to his car to get something out of the trunk. "Troy, it looks like some kind of devise to ram a door with. Maybe they're not shooting; still, pray for him; I think he may have tried to kill himself."

"You call me back and give me an update, okay? I will be praying. Hang in there. God is in control ... Okay?"

"I know He is. Thanks, Troy."

After hanging up the phone, I noticed the sound of what I thought was gunfire had turned eerily quiet. *It's over ... they've either killed him, got killed themselves or they are in there talking to him.* I desperately wanted to go in the house to see what was going on, but the officers had told me to stay by the car, and I knew it was for a reason. I prayed for my dad's lost soul while I waited, and after ten to fifteen minutes had passed by, an ambulance arrived. One of the police officers came out of the house to update me on the situation. "He did it."

"What do you mean, he did it?"

"He tried, but I think he missed. He took a knife and stabbed himself in the sternum. Unless he hit the liver, it's nothing but a gut wound that will probably heal up after the doctors' work on him." *I should have gone back for the knives.* The paramedics worked on dad in the house for over twenty minutes until he was finally wheeled out on a gurney.

Dad always enjoyed staying up late talking when he had been drinking. Often times, the conversation would wind its way down the same road until we came to the topic of the day he walked the dirt road. At that point, dad would talk about the image that was implanted into his memory. An image we both knew he would love to forget, but he had turned the image into a proud war wound that he liked to show me. He would often say that I should see something like that someday, so I would know what it was like.

I always knew it was the alcohol talking. Sober dad would never say anything with such malice. But we live in a spiritual world that has an ongoing battle between good vs. evil. Everyone has a weakness, and the Enemy will use that weakness to destroy.

On April 22, 2012, the Enemy used Dad's weakness of drinking against me. As dad was being wheeled out on a gurney, an image of him lying on his back with a butcher knife protruding from his chest was forever implanted in my mind. I can see the image as clearly today as if I was standing there. However, my heart belongs to Christ. And there will be no bondage used against me as that image doesn't haunt me like the Enemy hoped it would. Instead, it serves as a daily reminder to never miss an opportunity to reach out to someone who is suffering and teach them about the love of Christ. Am I perfect at this? Absolutely not, I am human just like you, and I fail to share sometimes. However, my heart is right, and I strive daily to be better than the disciple I was yesterday.

Before the ambulance took dad away, one of the police officers came up to me and asked if I wanted to speak to dad. At first, I did. I wanted to let him know that everything was going to be okay. I wanted to tell him I was sorry for the way I had treated him in the past, how I should have tried to understand what he battled daily. But with each step I took towards dad, the more I thought about what I was living out and the anger began to flow through my veins. *You accomplished it dad. I now have that image you have always wanted me to have. How could you be so selfish? How could you not think about your grandkids? How am I going to tell my children, and how could you be so hateful to mom?* I don't know if dad knew I was there or not, but if he did, the remaining will to live he might have had was probably sucked out of him as I turned my back towards him and walked away. I told the police officer that it was best I not speak to him. I'm sure he was confused by my actions, but he didn't know the past dad and I share.

I knew walking away probably disappointed my Father in Heaven. I believe I was placed there to witness to dad one last time, and I can't help but feel that I let the Enemy win. Sometimes, it's hard being a Christian. Learning to set aside emotions of the world in order to advance God's kingdom is something that I am chasing. If I had it to relive, I would pray to Jesus to help me climb inside the ambulance to speak life into my dad. Knowing now the time with him in the ambulance would be the last time I would see him conscious, I wish I would have stayed and spent it telling him once more about the cross while praying for his salvation.

Dad was airlifted to a hospital where the doctors were able to operate on his flesh wound. He came in without any identification and was listed as a John Doe. When we arrived, we were told they did not have anyone under his name. However, they said a male that was airlifted in from Cullman was in surgery and they probably had not updated the system. We were told to wait in the surgery waiting area and someone would eventually come out and speak to us. Three hours had passed before a doctor finally arrived and informed us that he was in ICU for recovery.

For the next eleven days, my family prayed hard for complete healing … but sometimes the answer is no. The knife wound closed up and healed fine during his stay in the ICU, but due to many health problems, which were unknown to any of us, Dad lost his eleven day battle on May 4th 2012. Although the death certificate relates his death to health related problems, I know it was the wound that never healed from so many years ago that really killed him.

The memorial service to celebrate his life was held on May 6th at the church mom attended regularly while dad chose to turn away. For me, the day was filled with mixed emotions, and the only way I really knew how to cope was to praise our Lord for the good times I had with my dad. So I lifted my hands and worshipped a Father in Heaven who I knew would never leave my side.

The next few months were hard on us all. When tragedy strikes, it is difficult to overcome. You have to focus on Jesus and have a different perspective. We all knew that we could live our lives in two ways. We could mope around thinking negative thoughts and allow the Enemy to destroy us, or we could focus on

the good, share memories and speak life into one another. Me …
I didn't do a very good job at either. I was still angry that my dad
would be so selfish. I was angry that I didn't stay with him and
talk to him like he asked. I was angry that I had to see him on
the gurney with a knife protruding from his chest. But most of
all, I was angry at the fact that he could not stop drinking. He
would have never mustered up the courage to do what he did had
he not been drinking.

No one knew how full of rage I was towards him and the
whole situation. I knew that I had to free myself from the burden
of guilt and anger. I needed to forgive my dad, but at the time,
I wasn't ready. I wanted to hold onto all the anger toward him.
I don't know why, but it just felt right. That's how the Enemy
manipulates and lies. Something I should do for God sometimes
feels odd … like forgiving the person that hurt you the most. That
is hard to do, but holding onto the anger is easy and feels normal.
I was tricked and was no better than my dad. There were two
gates that I could have chosen. One opened the way to a path of
forgiveness, mercy and love. The other led the way to a path of
hate, guilt and regret. The Enemy had gained a little control over
me, which clouded my ability to choose the gate which led to the
path to Christ.

I was on my way home from a business trip in Mississippi
when this all hit me. I decided to take a detour to the church,
which took me forty minutes out of my way, but it was worth it.
When I pulled into the church parking lot, I was happy to see
that no one else was there. Joy began to come upon me as I kept
thinking, *all of this ends today; it's ending today.* I walked into the
sanctuary and down the aisle that led me to the altar. I hit my
knees as tears filled my eyes and begged Jesus to take it away. I
asked for forgiveness for living in anger, I confessed all of my sins
and forgave my dad. Immediately, I felt different. The heaviness
inside of me was gone. The anger and bitterness was replaced with

a sense of joy and happiness. I thanked Jesus for what he did for us on the cross and left the church a changed man.

God works in miraculous ways, but it takes faith to truly see what God can do. I doubted God for years in my life and have come to the understanding that I am not in control. There are some things in life that only God can handle. If you don't learn to have faith and believe in Jesus with all your heart, the burdens of the world will rob you from blessings and steal the life God has planned for you. Jeremiah 29:13, Deuteronomy 4:29 and Psalms 119:1 all mention how we can find God if we are searching for Him by seeking Him with our whole hearts. To understand God's love and power, you cannot second guess or question His existence, which takes a lot of faith. You have to trust and not question.

I analyze everything, including the existence of God. This became an object the Enemy would use against me as I tried to walk with Christ. It took me a long time to stop analyzing the probability and reality that God exists. I battled with doubt and snickered at the thought of miraculous healing. It took diving into ministry along with years of being surrounded by pastors who spoke life into me and lived their lives as examples of Christ before I finally quit trying to justify how God exists and replaced analyzing with faith. I began committing myself to Christ daily, and God began to show up. My eyes saw things in a new way. My ears heard pain and suffering from words that used to be viewed as griping and complaining. Things of the past that didn't make sense became clear to me as I looked back on my entire life and saw the evidence of God's existence. I could see how He was there for me when I thought I was all alone. I was full of faith and chasing God became my passion.

Unemployed

❦

Nearly two years to the date after dad chose to end his life, I lost my job. My dismissal came on the heels of the best year of my fifteen years in sales. To add more confusion, for the past three years I had more sales and growth than anyone in the company. I could not comprehend why I was being let go. In my mind, there was no explanation for the decision. I struggled with trying to make since of why this was happening until I reached a level of frustration and knew that Troy might offer some wisdom that could help me gain a new perspective. I'm a proud man and really didn't want to let on to the fact that I was hurting so deeply. But I needed closure and decided to bring it up in a casual conversation one day. Troy reminded me, sometimes when life doesn't make sense, God's involved. I agreed and tried to find a new perspective. I told myself that I must trust God as He has it all planned out, but like I said earlier … being a Christian is hard.

Most days I felt good about my circumstance and found the peace that Jesus offered, but some days I would hold on to the worldly ways and allow the Enemy to sneak in filling me with anger and bitterness. I am human and fall extremely short of Christ, but have learned if I can avoid opening the wrong gate, I will find the path from God in the midst of chaos.

Years ago, I would have turned to the bottle to comfort my pain, but I had learned to steer my focus in a new direction.

When I would begin to think "why me," which could have led to self-destruction, I turned my energy to something that helped me connect with Jesus.

Living in an old house has its positives and its negatives. One of the negatives is having a lot of projects. There is always something to fix or a room that needs to be gutted and remodeled. In turn, this was also a positive during the times I needed to connect with Christ. You see, Jesus was a carpenter, and when I'm building things, I feel more connected with Him. During the months of April, May and June, a lot of projects were completed. When I was not spending time searching for a job, I was spending time with God in my garage, which was being used more for storage and my workshop. There were many times during those three months that I asked God what He had planned for me. I would beg for a clue or a sign, but I always came up empty. I tried hard to retain my thoughts from thinking about the things I could not control and tried harder to keep my emotions intact, but I am human. I would hold tight to Psalms 46:10, which says to be still and know that He is God. However, nothing made sense and by the end of May, I had grown restless. I began to plead for God to send me something for understanding, which He did in a way I will never forget.

—————◆◆◆—————

It was the first week in June 2014, Tamika was away visiting her parents with our kids and I was walking our dog, Trooper in the front yard when something came to my mind. It was almost like a voice, but not audible. Some may call it a vision but I didn't actually "see" anything. God speaks to us in many ways and one of them is by using our thoughts. However, not all our thoughts are from God and I certainly did not connect this one with Him as in my mind, this thought did not have a happy ending. *"What are you going to do when your wife is gone? How are you going to take care of all the flowers she has spent so much of her time on? It is a lot of work you know, but she loves them and you need to watch over them when she is gone.*"

Honestly, I didn't like the possible meaning of my thought and tried blow it off as if it never came to me. I hesitated to even mention it to anyone because I didn't want them thinking I was crazy … that is until Tamika found herself in the local emergency room.

Prepare

ᴥ

I cannot begin to tell you how much I love Tamika. I am addicted to her, and like an addict craves his next hit, I crave being with her. This addiction began the day we first kissed, but like an addict, I became complacent in my surroundings. I began taking advantage of my accessibility to my addiction. I lost respect and stopped being aware of her needs. In turn, I almost drove her away. But along the way, I found what I was missing. Clarity was brought back into my life, and I was awakened to the reality of how you are supposed to treat the one you love, which saved our marriage.

From there, God has used tragedies to bond us closer than ever before. We continued to hold tight to the vows we said, and by doing so, our marriage now stands on solid ground. But in the summer of 2011 a doctor noticed an arrhythmia on her heart that created uncertainty in regards to our plans to grow old together on the front porch swing.

An EKG was ordered which resulted in good news. We were told that her heart was fine and not to worry about it. He explained to us how some arrhythmias are life-threatening while others are nothing more than a part of our everyday life. I still had my concerns, but over the next three years, two other doctors picked up on her arrhythmia and ran tests that confirmed what we were told the time before.

On Monday, June 9, 2014, I took a flight to Rhode Island for an early morning interview on June 10th, while Tamika stayed home with the kids. Outside of me feeling as if I had blown my interview, everything went well during my trip. It wasn't until 8:00 the evening I returned from my trip when ours lived began to change forever.

Tamika and I were lying on the couch discussing our time away from one another when she developed a pain in her chest. It started out mild and would go away when she sat up, so I figured she had some heartburn, but after a Nexium did not help I began to wonder about the arrhythmia. I tried to get her to go to the hospital that night, but she insisted that it was not severe enough and thought some rest my help so we decided to go to bed. During the night, her moaning in pain woke me and I asked if she needed to go to the hospital. She insisted it was not that severe and took some aspirin to help ease the pain.

When she woke, the pain was continuous, and we knew she had to see a doctor immediately. Immediately, my mind raced back to the arrhythmias. I tried to use the knowledge regarding the EKG and what each doctor had told us to keep me calm during our ride to the hospital, but thoughts of a heart attack kept crossing my mind.

Could they have been wrong this entire time? Surely not; there have been at least three different doctors that came up with the same diagnosis. Besides, how could she be having a heart attack? She is only thirty-five and in great shape. She eats healthily and has never had high blood pressure. In fact, she has always run on the low side. It can't be a heart attack ... or could it?

When we pulled up to the ER, she could barely move without moaning in pain. They took her in and began placing wires all over her chest to monitor her heart. The wires running everywhere took me back to how Mandolyn looked when she spent her first eleven days in the NICU; followed by the image of my dad lying in the ICU where he spent his last twelve days before passing away. Our family had been through a lot in the past two years, and I had grown to love my wife more than ever. I couldn't allow her to see me weak during this time. I did my best to gather my composure before I walked to the bed to hold her hand.

"You're going to be all right." I told her while fighting off the tears. I wish I could say that I believed those words, but the thought I had a couple of weeks before told me differently. As I held her soft hand, I wondered if the heart condition had finally caught up with her.

In attempt to keep from crying, I turned away from Tamika and focused on the monitor that displayed the results in waveform patterns. I'm sure I appeared to be a little arrogant by the way I was studying the monitor as if I knew what I was looking at. I began probing the nurse for answers to what this meant and what that meant. She was aware of my concern and reassured me that her heart was fine. On the other hand, more tests were being ordered. I thanked her as she left the room.

It was not long after the nurse left when they arrived with the X-Ray machine, which revealed some fluid around her heart. This led the team to believe she had pericarditis, which is an effusion of the pericardial fluid around the heart. A CT scan was ordered to see if they could get a better idea of what exactly was going on.

Glancing at the clock, I knew it was almost time for our three daughters to be picked up from cheer practice. We had made arrangements for someone to take them earlier that morning but they were not able to bring them home. All morning, I had tried to get them a ride home but never was able to make it happen. Reluctant to leave, I slowly leaned over the bed rail, kissed my wife, told her I loved her and that everything was going to be okay before walking out the door to get the girls.

During the time I was gone, the doctors decided to run an ultrasound on Tamika's heart to rule out any pericardial fluid effusions. After all results came back from each test, the doctor was ready to share what he had found. As he entered the room, he asked Tamika if I were in the hospital.

"No, he has left to pick up our girls from cheer practice."

"Okay. It's probably best if he's not here anyway." Knowing that the news he was about to share with her merited a tender delivery, he reached down and held her hand gently. "Mrs. Powell, you have a mass in your chest that is causing all the pain. We will be admitting you tonight for observation and performing the biopsy tomorrow. I wish you the best and will be praying for you." After the doctor left the room, tears began to pour down her face as she sobbed uncontrollably.

Things at home kept robbing me of my time, and I became frustrated when I realized that it had been an hour and a half since I had left the hospital. Every minute that passed was a minute spent thinking of her and what was causing so much pain. Finally, I made it back to the hospital, and by the smeared massacre along with the pale look on her face, I realized I had not been with her when she needed me the most. My heart sank and a lump went straight to my throat. She asked if I had seen the doctor, which I had not, and she knew that I would have questions, so we asked for him to come back to her room. When he gave me the report, I was taken aback by his news and didn't have a reaction other than verifying that her heart was okay.

The pain medicine kept Tamika heavily sedated over the next sixteen hours leaving me time alone to think about our life together and what our future would look like. Tamika had always brought balance to my life, and I needed her to be there with me on that front porch swing to maintain that balance. After making arrangements for the kids I focused on getting the word out to people who would pray for her. I knew this was out of my control, and we needed God to perform a miracle.

The next day, Tamika was taken to another part of the hospital for the biopsy. During her entire absence, I prayed that everything would go smoothly and the results would come back negative. I told God how much I loved my wife and how I needed her to be here with me. I wished that I could have taken her place, but I couldn't. All I could do was trust that God would hear and answer my prayers. An hour had passed before they brought her back to the room. The nurse told us that she would rest for a few hours, and then we would be released. Tamika was still in severe pain, but we were told by the nurse that it was probably from the biopsy, and the pain should go away after a day or two. Judging by the look on Tamika's face, I knew she was not ready to go home and should have spoken up, but I kept silent, trusted their opinions and took her home.

By the next morning, Tamika could not move her face an inch without pain striking her chest. Suddenly, she began to vomit over and over, so I contacted the doctor who told me to bring her back immediately. Getting Tamika to the car was a slow, challenging process. She was unable to walk on her own, and each stop sent a wave of pain into her chest. The ride to the hospital was worse than the walk to the car. Every bump sent Tamika into pain and each curve sent a wave of nausea all over her. When we finally arrived at the hospital, another chest X-Ray was performed, and later that night the doctor informed us the fluid they saw yesterday was now in both lungs and she had pneumonia. Honestly, having to go back to the hospital after being released provoked concerns regarding the quality of care we were receiving, but during the doctor's visit, I realized how blessed we were to be under the care of a doctor who was willing to take as much time as he did to explain her condition.

Tamika was treated for three days in the hospital. Once the pain subsided and she was ready, they sent us home. Outside of knowing about the mass, Tamika was her old self again. She had neither pain nor any other symptoms that signaled anything was wrong. Realizing the mass would have not been found without the pain, we thanked God for her developing pneumonia in the middle of June.

I was amazed to watch Tamika around the house as she appeared to be her old self again. She walked with grace and carried the beautiful smile that lights up the room. She appeared to be just as healthy as ever. But we both were very much aware of the mass that pushed against her heart while forcing her left lung out three centimeters creating anxiety like none we had ever faced before. My way of dealing with anxiety is usually done in front of the computer researching possible solutions. Tamika always went to the flower beds to deal with anxiety. Pulling weeds and deadheading the flowers, seemed to always bring some sort of peace to Tamika. Since I have known her, she has loved being outdoors, especially when it came to making things pretty. But on this day, pulling the weeds had much more meaning. She saw them as the threat they were to her flowers just as the mass was the threat to her life. Each weed pulled was symbolic to removing the mass that was threating her life.

Normally, I would complain about how much time and money was being spent on flowers. In return, she would always tell me the time in the yard was peaceful to her as it brought her closer with God. But this time, I did not complain at all. My wife was sick, and I had no idea what the future held. As far as I was concerned, she could have stayed in the yard all night long. I needed her to be away from me for a while anyway. I wanted to be strong and positive, but the thought I had two weeks prior was now haunting me and kept running through my mind over and over and over.

As I pushed my faith aside by assembling my own plan to attack the worst if needed, Tamika's faith grew stronger. Right at dusk, she came inside with a bright smile on her face that glowed with confidence.

"Cliff, while I was pulling weeds, God reminded me that Deuteronomy 31:8 tells us not to worry. He has gone before me and has laid the path for me. He reminded me that He will never leave me nor forsake me. Cliff, it says to not be afraid nor be discouraged. I know that no matter what, I am going to be okay."

Her faith was contagious, and I was ashamed that I had backslid and not shared the same faith. I put down the computer and gave her a hug and a kiss. "You're right. We have to trust Him. This is out of our hands, and we must rely on Him to get us through this season of our life."

The next seven days were spent in the land of the unknown, which kept me on edge. Each time one of us would lose sight of God, the other was there to bring focus where it belonged. When the call finally came in, we listened carefully as the doctor shared the news of her preliminary results. I will never forget the words Diffused Large B-Cell Lymphoma, a very aggressive cancer that called for immediate attention. However, this was preliminary and we were told they needed more tissue to complete the tests. There was one more type they needed to rule out before writing an official report. In order to pull more tissue, Tamika would have to undergo an invasive surgery.

Our doctor was able to get us in with the best thoracic surgeon in the southeast. However, ten days would go by before he could see us and then another few days before surgery would take place. With the words very aggressive cancer along with the vision I had from earlier that month, I was not going to sit back and let the tumor gain ground on the woman I planned spending the rest of my life with. A CT scan was performed on her the prior October in preparation for an upcoming parathyroid surgery. Tamika thought it might show the mass if there was one during that time. We were not for certain if it would or not, but our curiosity encouraged us to make the forty five minute drive to pick up the results.

During the drive, we discussed our options and focused on speaking positive words to encourage one another. When we arrived at the hospital, Tamika went inside to collect the disc as I waited in the car. During my wait, I said and prayer asking God to direct my steps. As soon as I finished the prayer, I remembered that I was going to call Vanderbilt Medical Center as they were one of the top three in the nation for Lymphoma.

While the phone was ringing, I prayed for them to have an opening and be willing to see her.

As Tamika returned to the car, I was still on the phone hoping for a prayer to be answered. The receptionist kept me waiting while she communicated offline to see if they could work us in. When she came back, I expected an answer, but instead I was teased by another question about her age and preliminary diagnosis. It was another five minutes until she came back to me with an appointment for the upcoming Tuesday. I pulled onto an exit to take down some notes regarding what to bring, appointment times and the logistics upon our arrival. As we were pulled over, five police cars flew passed us. A minute or two later, two ambulances flew by. It appeared they all headed towards the airport. Curious to know what was going on, Tamika turned on the radio to surf the stations for information, but nothing was reported. It wasn't until later in the drive home that we learned about the small plane that had crashed taking the lives of all three on board. All of the sudden, our situation had a new perspective.

Five hours after scheduling the appointment with Vanderbilt, the phone rang with Tamika's sister on the other end. She was calling to let us know that her brother-in-law was able to get us an appointment with an oncologist the next morning at eleven. Turns out he had some connections and called them up at 8:00 p.m. in hopes to get her in ASAP. We were humbled by God's love and astonished at how we could see Him working. I was convinced that Tamika did hear from God and that He did have a path laid for us.

Tamika received her preliminary diagnosis on June 18th. We met with the local oncologist Thursday morning June 19th. A PET scan was performed on Friday, June 20th. On Monday, June 23rd we met with a thoracic surgeon to discuss surgery that would take place on Thursday, June 26th. On, Tuesday the 24th, we met with the specialist at Vanderbilt and learned surgery was not needed. He assured us that she had Primary Mediastinal Large B-Cell Lymphoma, which is a subtype of Diffused Large B-cell. He went on to tell us they use the same treatment (R-EPOCH) on both. Schedule-wise, we learned what the next four months of our life would look like.

On Wednesday, June 25th a bone marrow biopsy was performed. If the results from the biopsy came back negative, then Tamika's life would soon consist of be admitted to the hospital for 5-6 days followed by coming home for two weeks to only return again on the third week for another round of chemo. There were a total of six rounds with a PET scan after the fourth to see how effective the plan was working. He gave us the option to get started as soon as she liked but no later than July 1st. Tamika and I looked at each other and both agreed to begin June 30th which was the upcoming Monday. We had been on the go ever since we learned the preliminary diagnosis and needed time to spend with the kids. They needed to hear from us what was going on with their mom and how this would be affecting their lives. God had already worked many miracles just in the scheduling department, especially in the caregiver's schedule. I was now beginning to understand the blessing God had given us by taking away the job I loved. But God had a lot of work to do if he was planning on replacing the significant amount of income loss that went along with the job. Overall, I was thankful to still be unemployed and was one hundred percent dedicated to caring for my wife.

The thought I had earlier in the month still haunted me every day. Tamika and I were dedicated to speaking life into our situation, so telling her about it was not an option. But I needed to understand what it meant. *Was it nothing to worry about? I don't think so ... it was too real. Was it the Enemy just messing with me? No. I don't think he speaks to us in ways like that. It must be God preparing me then. But why would he prepare me for the death of my wife?* I just didn't get it. I needed someone rooted in their faith; someone that could explain to me what it meant as it was driving me crazy.

I knew I needed an answer before she started her first round of treatment, and time was not on my side. At the time, one of our neighbors was a great friend of mine as well as married to my third cousin. Often times, he and I would accidentally meet up while taking trash to the road, which always led to a conversation. Being a Christian, as well as a person who could think in depth, he would be the perfect person to ask. I guess it was the Saturday before treatment started when he walked over to check on Tamika. When he left, I made a point to walk out with him and probed him for his thoughts on my vision that kept haunting me.

As I listened to his interpretation, clarity began to come to life. The urgency was the focus. God was preparing me to not sit back and wait. Had we blown off her pain or waited on the thoracic surgeon in place of calling Vanderbilt, she might not have made it. All my decisions were based on not waiting due to the vision I had in early June. Relief came over me and a couple of weeks later, Troy's wife, Kelly confirmed it by with her interpretation that matched nearly word for word.

Round One

When someone is diagnosed with a life threatening illness, there are two ways to look at it. You can choose to wallow in self-pity, or you can choose to focus on the blessings that come along with the diagnosis. I know the Enemy very well, and if given the chance, he will use self-pity every time to destroy you and everything around you. Tamika and I knew that it was critical that we keep our focus on the blessings. We began speaking life into the season we were in, which brought us hope as well as a perspective of choosing life over death. We chose to not look at cancer as a negative life ending disease; instead, we chose to see it as an opportunity to make a difference. We wanted to use our journey as a life changing one that would have meaning at the end. At the time, we were not sure exactly what that would look like, but it was our prayer.

Shortly after the mass was found, I began sending out text blasts updating everyone and requesting specific prayers. The time it consumed became too much, and I knew I must change my way of communicating with our prayer team. I decided to create a group on Facebook and named it Pray for Tamika Powell. It didn't take long for her group to reach over a thousand people. The amount of support we received was simply amazing. God works through the unity of prayer and I'm convinced one reason she was doing so well emotionally was due to God honoring the prayers from the large number of people speaking life into her day and night.

I wanted to have a special day where people could come together and pray over Tamika before she left for her first round of treatment. I scheduled an event for her prayer group to meet at our church at 3:00 p.m. the Sunday before her treatments would begin. At the time, we had around three hundred members on her Facebook prayer group, and I expected around fifty to show, but that number was doubled. Tamika and I were both humbled by the generosity. We had friends and family members drive from hours away to pray for her. She was able to see some of her friends that she had not seen in over twelve years. We felt very blessed, and it was just what Tamika needed to prepare her for the next day.

On the way to Nashville, Tamika was focused and anxious to begin. Knowing that she was determined to win this battle and could not wait to get it behind her helped me have peace. When we pulled up to the clinic to check in, I looked at her and told her how proud I was that she was my wife. We said a prayer and walked to the receptionist's desk to get a copy of her schedule for the day. Tamika started out with labs followed by her PICC line placement then to meet with her oncologist and finally to admissions where we waited for seven hours for a room.

Labs were a breeze and nothing more than a routine needle to draw blood, but the PICC line was a different story. Tamika was a little apprehensive about getting the line, mainly because she was not sure what all it entailed. When they began the process of inserting the line, reality of what was about to take place hit, and Tamika's anxiety caught up with her. Later on, she explained the process of inserting the PICC, and I could see why it would be overwhelming. "Is it painful?" I asked.

"No, it was just the thought of it running through my veins and making its way to my heart. Then it took a turn and tried to run up my throat. They said it was normal and showed me what to do to close the flap so it would turn down."

"Man, that sounds scary."

"Now that I know what to expect, it probably won't be as bad the next time."

"Probably not," I said as we walked into the clinic to meet with the oncologist. After we finished at the clinic, we grabbed some lunch and then headed to admissions.

"You're going to love the tenth floor," we were told by several different people at the hospital. Tamika's response was always the same. "I hope; we are supposed to be on vacation right now. We had to cancel a pre-paid trip to Cancun because of this." The seven hour wait for a room was the hardest part of the day.

When her name was finally called by a man from transport, we gathered our luggage, and Tamika sat in the wheelchair. Finally, we were on our way to the tenth floor, only the button the man pushed was eleven.

"Are we not on the tenth floor?"

"The paper tells me eleven sir." I looked at Tamika and could tell she was concerned, so I asked if eleven is as good as ten. "Ten is new and much nicer, but you will be happy with eleven as well." I looked at Tamika again, and she gave me a look of doubt and I could feel her disappointment. When we arrived at our room, Tamika almost began to cry. She was very upset and felt misled. We both had hoped for a large room that made you feel at home, but reality was, we were in a hospital and not Cancun. We made an attempt to get moved to the tenth floor, but it didn't work out, which later we were thankful for.

As we met the nurses, we learned the disappointment in our room was now camouflaged by the personalities of our nurses. They were funny, kind and really helped take the edge off. After being there for a few hours, we agreed the most important part was the quality of care and not the room.

Surprisingly to me, the week of treatment flew by fast, and Tamika didn't have many side effects. I kept asking the nurses what we should expect during two weeks at home. But they all said chemo affects everyone differently, but it's mostly flu-like symptoms: excessive drowsiness, nausea, along with aches and pains. On Saturday, they called in four prescriptions to our local pharmacy and sent us home. She had completed round one.

Visits to the ER

✎

The ride home was a little rough on Tamika. She was nauseas but never got sick. "It comes in waves," she told me.

"Try to close your eyes and rest. We'll be home soon." The ride home took the normal two hours, and although she felt fine most the time, I could tell a difference in Tamika. She slept fine all night and woke up the next day feeling like herself. Around ten o'clock, I went to the pharmacy to pick up the medicines waiting on her. "What are these?" I asked the pharmacist.

"One is for gastrointestinal issues, one is an antibiotic, one is an antiviral and the other is an antifungal. It appears that they are all prescribed for preventative measures."

"Probably so; she just completed her first round of chemo and is prone to catching anything."

"I hope everything goes well with her treatments."

"Thank you," I said as I walked away.

It was around 10:30 a.m. when I walked through our door. Tamika was sitting on the front porch, so I headed into the kitchen and poured her something to drink to go along with the pills. By the time noon rolled around, her stomach was burning, and she decided to lie down in bed until it went away. I knew I had thirty more minutes before I could give her the Prilosec, or it would interact with the Levaquin. But her stomach was burning pretty bad, so I tried giving her some ice cream, hoping it would help soothe the burning. The ice cream was not effective nor was the Prilosec. I began to wonder if this pain was due to chemotherapy. The nurses had mentioned body aches and flu like symptoms; however, no one said anything about burning in the abdomen. Although, they did say chemo affects everyone differently.

Throughout the afternoon, sharp stabbing pains throughout her body began to accompany the burning in her abdomen. Tamika was very uncomfortable and I knew it was time to make a trip to the ER. We grabbed the items we needed and slowly walked Tamika to the car. Once again, it was a slow ride to the hospital. Knowing how Tamika felt, I took each turn carefully and tried my best to avoid every bump along the way. When we finally arrived, they started an IV for fluids and got her a dose of Dilaudid for the pain. I am not sure if it was the pain medicine or the chemo, but for the first time, Tamika got sick. They ran labs on her and performed an X-Ray for precautionary purposes. I was on the phone with Vanderbilt doctors and requesting information on what to look for in the lab work.

At 9:30 p.m. the doctor returned with the results we had been waiting on. After conversing with Vanderbilt's doctors everyone was in agreement that there was no reason for her to be admitted. Before letting her go home, they gave her one more round of dilaudid and a potassium pill. The dilaudid knocked Tamika out of it for the ride home, but as we pulled into the driveway she began to feel nauseous again. "I'm going to throw up, hand me the bag."

"I can't find one; just stick your head out the door." After getting her a wet washrag to clean her with, I eased Tamika into the house and put her to bed. She moaned and groaned in pain until 2:00 a.m. and I kept thinking to myself, *surely chemo does not cause this much pain.* We had talked to a lot of people that had been through cancer, and no one had ever mentioned sharp stabbing pains and burning throughout their bodies. But none of them had taken the R-EPOCH regimen either, so once again, I was left with trusting the doctors.

The following day, we were scheduled to see her local oncologist for labs at 3:30. I wish I would have rescheduled that appointment for earlier in the morning, but for some reason I didn't. I guess it was due to the fact that we had been prescribed Norco for pain and Nystatin for mouth sores leaving me thinking that we could manage the pain and dehydration at home. Besides, when Tamika woke up around 7:00 that morning, she felt fine. I gave her the first round of her medicine at 7:30 and the second round at 10:30. By the time it was almost noon, Tamika was in pain again. The pain this time was more severe than the last. I kept thinking to myself, *this cannot be from the chemo treatment,* so I contacted Vanderbilt again, and they reassured me that it affects everyone differently, and sometimes it causes more pain than other times. "Just keep on top of it with the Norco, and let her local oncologist know everything going on during your appointment today; however, chemo can cause motion sickness, so I will call in a patch that you will apply behind her ear for three days. If the nausea persists after three days, apply one more but no more after that. You call back if both rounds do not work. Okay?" I told the doctor okay and hung up the phone.

Tamika was not moving since the world started spinning if she did, and I could not leave her, so I got my mom to go pick up the patch for me. As soon as mom returned with it, I applied it to the appropriate location. The motion sickness eased up a little, but the pain trumped the sickness and left Tamika still feeling nauseous. I kept looking at the clock hoping to speed up time. I longed for her appointment time, hoping they would have ideas to improve her situation. When 2:30 rolled around, it was time to make the forty minute trip to her local oncologist. Upon arrival, I took Tamika in on a wheelchair, and they immediately ran an IV to get her hydrated.

An admission to the hospital was recommended for evaluation. The oncologist informed us that we would be under the care of the hospitalist but close enough her oncologist could check in on Tamika daily. We agreed that would be best and began the process. Once Tamika was in her room, the nurses had to run a new IV. Of course by now, Tamika was sick of IV's and looked at me with the eyes of an injured puppy. After the IV was in place, they gave her a 2 mg dose of Dilaudid to help with the pain. For the next three days, her regular medicines prescribed by Vanderbilt were administered along with Dilaudid every four hours. Even after all the medicine, Tamika lay in the hospital in pain. Each day the pain grew more intense, and she needed Dilaudid more frequently. I didn't understand what could be causing this pain and kept hammering both oncologists for explanations. However, each time I asked, the answer was the same, "chemo affects everyone differently." Unwilling to accept their answer, I decided to turn to God to take away her pain.

Sometimes God answers prayer immediately, other times may take years before you see evidence of His work, and sometimes, the answer is no. However, Matthew 18:19 says that if two agree on earth it will be done by our Father in Heaven, so I believe the more people are united in prayer, the more God is moved to act. While Tamika slept off the nightmare called pain, I updated her Facebook group asking for everyone to agree with me in prayer then began to pray hard for the pain to be taken away.

Dilaudid is stronger than morphine and knocked her out to the point where she was not able to make rational decisions. Nevertheless, the following day while I went out to get us some lunch, the doctor allowed her to make a decision to get a port. When I returned, Tamika looked over at me with the eyes of a stoner and said, "I'm getting a port."

"What!?"

"I'm getting a port tomorrow. I signed for it and everything." Tamika and I had discussed a port before being admitted for her first round, and she was set against a port.

"Are you sure you want a port? Remember, Vanderbilt pushed for the PICC line so there must be a reason they prefer it over the port. Besides, I thought you had decided to not get a port. What made you change your mind?"

"Everyone here keeps suggesting that I get one. So, I did." Knowing that she was not in the right mindset to make that decision, I was shocked that they would even allow her to sign off on it.

"I'll contact Vanderbilt and get their take on it. I am sure you can cancel if you decide to."

"Okay," she said in a carefree voice.

I researched and contacted many nurses that I knew, and most said to go with a port, but Vanderbilt's nurse made a point about still being stuck many times unless you have a double lumen port. This stuck in my mind as well as brought reasoning and a new perspective. But it was her sister Rene who convinced me that a port this late in the game was not the way to go. Rene is a cancer survivor, and she loved her port when she was going through chemo, but her recovery from the port placement surgery was not as easy as they made it out to be.

"Cliff, I had a two or three week recovery and was in some pain during that time. I think Tamika just needs to go with the PICC line and forget about getting a port. I also feel like the risks outweigh the benefits. Tamika is already in a lot of pain, and her body is so weak. If they put in a port right now, it might create a downward spiral. That is not what she needs right now."

"I agree, Rene. I'll tell Tamika what you've told me, and I'm sure we will be cancelling the surgery."

"Tell her, I love her too."

"I will. Thank you for the advice."

After she said bye, I hung up the phone and told Tamika everything she said. Tamika was so out of it; I'm not sure it even registered, but she agreed to cancel the surgery, so I called the nurse in immediately and the appointment was cancelled.

Our nurse on Wednesday night missed her calling. She was not nurse material at all. Very frustrated at the fact that Tamika's IV monitor kept going off, she became quite short with Tamika and said, "You are going to have to stop moving around. The placement of the IV is causing the machine to go off over and over when you move."

Tamika told her she would try, but she couldn't help it because she itched all over. It was 1:15 a.m. when the nurse came in for the fifth time to fix the machine. Only this time, she brought with her another IV. "I am going to try an IV in the hand since the one in the arm isn't working. But just in case the one in the hand does not work, I will leave the one in the arm in so we can go back to it."

Had I not been so sleepy and dosing in and out of sleep while this was going on, it might have registered how ridiculous it was.

Basically, she was going to stick my wife again just to keep her from having to do her job. At 2:55 a.m. I woke up to groans of pain coming from Tamika. She was in tears and said her hand hurt. I looked at it, and it looked like a golf ball had been implanted under her skin where the IV was placed. Frustrated, I buzzed the nurse and told her she needed to check on the IV as it was swollen. The nurse huffed and puffed as she took the IV out of Tamika's hand and placed it back in to the one she had left in her arm.

The Dilaudid must have worn off because Tamika buzzed the nurse again in pain around 4:00 a.m. After giving Tamika the medicine, the nurse informed her that she gave her four mg instead of the two mg she had been receiving. "Why?" Tamika asked.

"Because 2 mg was just not lasting long enough, and you need more to help you rest."

Thursday morning is when the mumbling in her sleep began. It started with Tamika constantly scratching herself while asleep and then turned into mumbling while scratching. Around midday, the hospitalist came in and discussed sending us home. Tamika protested as she was scared to go home still in so much pain. She had been in and out of the ER two times already and admitted to the hospital for pain, which had only intensified over the past three days. She asked him why she couldn't stay to which he replied that he could not justify her being there to the insurance company as he turned to walk out the door.

After settling down a little, Tamika grew hungry and wanted a Strawberry Pop Tart from a vending machine, so I left the room in search for one. Normally, Tamika would not have been specific as to a flavor, but chemo affects the taste buds and I knew that I needed to return with what she requested. Determined to find the Strawberry, I walked all over that hospital but to my disappointment, every machine was out and I had to settle for a Blueberry flavor from the Coffee Shop. While I was out, the hospitalist had visited Tamika again this time in an almost accusatory way asking questions that she was not comfortable with, upsetting her to the point where she wanted to leave ASAP. I agreed that it was time for us to go and packed up our things, completed our paperwork and headed home.

One of the main concerns her doctors stressed was the lowering of her immune system due to the reduction in a type of white blood cell. This is referred to as being neutropenic. It is temporary, however when she was neutropenic, the last place she needed to be was in the ER. The only time you want to go there is if you have no other option. Tamika's pain was very intense and we were out of options. Mentally, she was drained and could not take much more. Thoughts of ruptured organs raced through her mind while the pain shot all throughout her body. She was scared and without the security of being in the hospital she began to think the worst. I tried to calm her down and assured her that nothing had ruptured, but she was not convinced. I knew she needed to calm her nerves, or she was going to send herself into a panic attack. The only option I knew of was to make another trip to the ER. When we arrived, Tamika's labs were run confirming she was neutropenic. The ER doctor ordered an X-Ray as well as a CT scan to rule out any possible issues inside her abdomen. When everything came back normal, her nerves calmed down tremendously.

We were released to go home, and she took her last pain pill at 11:30 before falling asleep for the night. One thing I learned from the ER doctor was that the Prilosec worked better if taken at night, so after Tamika fell asleep, I rearranged the times I would give her medicine. The new medicine schedule left an isolated dose of Levaquin to be taken at 10:00 a.m. instead of being taken with all the other medicines. When Tamika woke up the next morning, she felt normal, and for the first time in five days got out of bed to walk around the house. At 11:00 a.m. that day, I remembered the Levaquin dose she was supposed to take an hour earlier. Forty-five minutes after taking the single pill, Tamika started burning in her stomach, which prompted her to ask, "What is the name of the pill I took?"

"Levaquin."

"I believe that is the medicine I took two years ago that you made me stop. Remember, Cliff? I was having pain and burning in my stomach, and you read the side effects. You got upset because they prescribed such a risky medicine to me when Amoxicillin had worked every other time before."

Tamika was right. I'm ashamed that I forgot about it. Our pharmacist confirmed that Levaquin was, in fact, the medicine she was prescribed. We told them to put it on her allergy list and never let her have it again.

Because it was Friday, I knew I must get in touch with all the doctors fast before they left for the day. I raced to the phone and contacted our local oncologist as well as the one at Vanderbilt.

Everyone was in agreement that the pain she had been suffering all week was due to a reaction to Levaquin. I sat and thought about what the next 10-16 hours would bring as Levaquin worked through her body one last time. I knew it was going to be rough, but I never thought it would land us in the ER fighting for her life.

Knocking on Death's Door

♪♪

Knowing what was about to occur, Tamika grew very anxious. Her mind began to drift away from positive thoughts allowing fear to set in. She began to second guess the medicine I was giving her, which creating an issue that I did not know how to handle. I tried to calm her down, but she only grew more frustrated with me, which created even less trust. At 12:30 p.m., a nurse from her local oncologist called to check in on Tamika to which I informed her about the anxiety. She recommended Ativan to aid in calming her nerves and had the doctor write out a prescription for us to pick up at the office.

Tamika's trust in me was gone and at first refused to ride with me to pick up the prescription, however after giving her some space, she agreed to go. I was careful to follow the doctors' orders regarding how to properly dose each medicine to prevent interactions, but when the mumbling started around 2:00 p.m., I wondered if I had messed up.

She would be asleep, then all of the sudden, she would begin to mumble some sort of sentence as if she had something important to say but could not get the words out. Within the next two hours, a sudden jerk appeared as if she was dreaming about falling and woke up, just before she hit the ground. Each time this would wake herself, she would moan out in pain and asked for more medicine. The Dilaudid could be taken every four hours, so I had to deny her request multiple times until it was time for another dose.

Earlier that week, we were told to stay ahead of the nausea. They said if she felt any sickness at all to go ahead and give her some medicine to keep her from getting to the point of throwing up and becoming more dehydrated. Zofran alone did not help her, so the doctors told us to follow it with Phenergan if needed. Tamika was very sick so I felt it was needed and began alternating medicines per doctors' orders. To control the nausea, she was receiving Phenergan every 8 hours, Zofran every 6, along with the patch she still had on from the hospital. The Phenergan was given first, followed with Zofran four hours later, then Phenergan again at the eight hour mark. It was the same routine everyone had been following throughout the week only this day Ativan was added to the mix. Between Dilaudid every four hours for pain, Ativan and all the nausea medicines, my wife was heavily medicated. I was well aware of the risks, however I felt as long as I kept in touch with both of her oncologists, all would be okay. Little did I know what was about to come.

About two hours after the second dose of Dilaudid, Tamika's mumbling turned into complete sentences. She would be reclining on the couch dozing off and talking as if someone were in the room. I was growing more and more concerned, but the doctors didn't seem to be alarmed unless she talked out of her head while awake. I would check her blood pressure every now and then to verify that she was not too low. Each time, it would check out to be fine. When 7:00 p.m. rolled around, Tamika was right on cue. She woke up moaning in pain. I tried to delay giving her anything for ten minutes, hoping she would fall back to sleep. This would have allowed more time between doses if it had worked, but the delay turned her moans into wailing that could be heard around the house. *What am I to do? She is very neutropenic, and if we go to the ER, she runs the risk of picking up an infection. Besides, they said last night she is safer at home than she is there due to the risk of infections.*

Another scream ran through the house like a flash of lighting. I could not stand to hear her in that much pain and decided that I had no option but to give her another dose of Dilaudid.

Tamika fell asleep once the pain medicine hit her system. Once again, she started making gestures while talking in her sleep. She would stick out her arm as if she was meeting someone while moving her hand up and down as if she was really shaking someone's hand. I remember one time she pointed up in the air and said "there it is, see it?" Another time she waved bye to someone and then suddenly jerked, which woke her up. She looked at me and asked if someone was there. I said no, and she told me that she thought she just saw someone standing right behind the couch. I told her that she had just waved bye to someone in her dream, and that is probably who she was thinking about.

At 9:30 p.m., I remembered that I told the owner of the repair shop to leave my key in the car after hours, and I would pick it up. *Crud, I can't leave Tamika here.* I called the neighbors and asked if they would mind helping me out. While on the phone with them, Tamika popped her head up from a dead sleep and asked me if I had given our dog his medicine.

"Tamika, he does not need medicine."

"Yes he does! He needs it in the morning and at night from the shots he received yesterday!"

"Tamika, baby, he has been at my brother's and has not even been at the vet this week." Realizing that she was wrong, Tamika burst out in tears wondering what was happening to her. I told my neighbor I had to go and walked over to where Tamika lay, and gently comforted her with prayer. By the time I was finished praying for her, she was asleep once more.

Although she was asleep, over the next two hours, the jerking and talking out of her head only got worse. As I stood there watching the involuntary movements her body was making, I thought about how time was quickly moving. *Soon the pain medicine will wear off. She will be screaming again, and I will need to give her another dose of pain medicine ... but I'm done with the Dilaudid. I need to call the oncologist and see what else she can take. I also need to let them know what's been going for the past two hours.*

When the doctor returned my call at 10:50 p.m., I informed her that Tamika had been talking out of her head, making gestures, and jerking involuntarily. I also provided her with the blood pressure readings. When I was done, she insinuated that I had provided good information. But what she said next was the difference in life or death for my wife. "If she appears to be awake while talking like that or if her respiratory rate drops below twelve breaths per minute, she needs to go to the ER immediately."

"Okay but what about more pain medicine. I don't want to give her more Dilaudid. Can I give her Percocet?"

"I doubt one Percocet will help with the pain, so give her one now, and if she is still in pain after thirty minutes, then give her one more. But that is all. No more than that until the four hours are up."

"Okay. Got it; thank you." The doctor was right. The 11:00 dose did not help at all. Tamika just laid in bed crying in pain until 11:30. I was thankful because the second pill did the trick. By 11:45, her crying had stopped. I went into the living room to log the type of medicine given along with what time it was given. By the time I came back into the bedroom, to my surprise, Tamika was up washing her face. I thought this was strange; however, she appeared to be going through her normal routine before she went to bed, so I decided to test her to see how she would respond.

"What are you doing babe?"

"I thought I would brush my teeth and wash my face before I went to sleep."

I studied her like a lion studies its prey. At this moment, I knew, outside of God intervening, her life was in my hands. After observing her for ten minutes, I was confident that Tamika appeared to be fine. The communicated constantly with her until she brought the pedicure set to the bed and began working on her feet. Although a little odd, this is not what alarmed me. It was her next question that sent my adrenaline into a near panic mode.

"Cliff, are you going to pick up the girls?"

I looked into my wife's gorgeous brown eyes and said, "I didn't hear you clearly, Tamika, can you ask your question again?"

"I am wondering if you are going to pick up the girls, or do I need to? I don't mind going to get them after I put on my shoes; I just need to know if that is what you want me to do."

My heart sank and I knew what had to be done. As I looked at Tamika, tears began rolling into my eyes, "Tamika, I love you so much. Tamika, do you know what time it is? It's almost midnight and our girls are at mom's next door spending the night. Tamika, the only place we need to go is the hospital. Will you ride with me to the Emergency Room?"

Tamika was hit hard when reality set in. She laid down screaming in tears wailing, "I don't know what's wrong with me! Why isn't my brain working right? I just want to be normal again!"

"Tamika, look at me … you are going to be fine, but we need to get going. Let's get your shoes on and go." I said a quick prayer over her and helped her off the bed.

As she stood to her feet and took her first few steps to the door, she asked, "Are you sure we need to go, Cliff? It is going to cost us another hundred and fifty dollars, and I could just crawl back in bed and fall asleep. I am really, really sleepy all of the sudden."

"Tamika, I'm absolutely sure; now let's go!" This was stated in a matter of fact way that left her with only one option: to go with me.

When we arrived, I told Tamika to wait in the car while I signed her in. Being that she was neutropenic, I wanted to keep her away from the waiting area as much as possible. I hopped out, went to the ER registration desk and proceeded to explain the urgent matter I was facing. "My wife has had a lot of pain medicine today. She has had, Phenergan, Zofran, Dilaudid, and

Percocet ... oh and Ativan. I think I may have overdosed her." Realizing what I was saying, I turned to the police officer sitting next to the receptionist and said, "But all of it has been given to her under doctor's orders." For a moment, I thought I might have been incriminating. During this time, it occurred to me that I had left the car running with Tamika, who was just talking about going to pick up our girls, in it alone.

Suddenly, I envisioned her driving down AL Hwy 157 crossing over the Lake Catoma bridge. *She might drive away! She has no idea what she is doing!* Without a word, I ran out of the door relieved to find my wife still in the passenger seat of the car. On the other hand, I was concerned that she had fallen asleep and was very difficult to wake up. The receptionist must have sensed my urgency as she followed me out with a wheelchair.

We were able to get Tamika out of the car and into the chair. The receptionist told me she would be in Triage as she rushed her in. After I parked the car, I met Tamika in a room in the ER. The nurse was hooking up the heart monitor and lead for respiratory.

Immediately, I looked for the RR on the monitor that would confirm what I had anticipated. *Only eight breaths per minute; my heart sank. She was hypo ventilating due to too much medicine. I nearly killed the one person that meant more to me than anything on earth.*

I gathered myself and walked the nurse through my day of struggles of trying to keep my wife comfortable. In a nice tone, the nurse said to just wait and tell it all to the doctor. Feeling out of breath and exhausted, I was glad to know that I did not have to run through the story twice.

When the doctor walked in, he touched Tamika's shoulder to check her response. There was not one at all, so he asked me what was going on. I proceeded to lay out the day I had battled as well as how the week had been for her. During my story, he had shook Tamika a few times in an attempt to get her to respond. It took a couple of efforts but she finally gave him a soft "huh?"

The doctor and nurse left the room, and I went over to Tamika, held her hand and told her I was sorry. I then, kissed my wife on the forehead and prayed over her life. I felt helpless, confused and angry. *How am I supposed to help my wife stay comfortable?"* About that time, the nurse came in with some medicine. She could see the concern in my face and reassured me she would be fine. "Usually when I give this medicine, the patients don't like me."

"What do you mean?"

"Well, when they wake up, they are angry and confused. They don't know what's going on and usually try to defend themselves."

"What is it?"

"It's called Narcan which is a drug that reverses the effects of the opiates."

When it dawned on me what she was saying I felt horrible. I really almost overdosed my wife and this was the confirmation that I really had almost killed my wife! Ugh!!! The frustration I had inside of me was raging higher and higher like a volcano preparing to explode.

I peeked at the monitor before the medicine was given and must have missed her giving it to Tamika. As I turned my head, she popped up and said, "Where am I and what is going on?" She was confused by her surroundings. The next sentence shocked me. "I did not take anything, HE GAVE IT ALL TO ME!" Pointing at me pleading her innocence to what she thought everyone was thinking was a suicide attempt. The nurse told her that everything was okay and she was brought in by me because I was concerned about the effects the medicine was having on her.

The next 4 hours Tamika and I spent fighting and yelling at each other in that room. Both of us were beaten down by the events of the week, which had led us to the brink of devastation. I was at my wits end, and Tamika was accusing me of almost killing her! Tamika threatened me with, "I'm going to my mom and dad's tomorrow, and they will take care of me." But I didn't care at that point and my response confirmed it.

"Good, I'm done with this anyway! Do you think this has been a fun day for me? Do you think it's fun trying to decide whether to watch your wife lie screaming in pain or give her the medicine she needs knowing that it could kill her? Let me answer it for you … it's not! So, if you think your parents can do a better job, then, call them and have them come get you. It's fine with me! I'm sick of this anyway!"

The Enemy knows our weaknesses. He knows how to twist and manipulate two happily married people into thinking they are just not meant to be together. However, we serve a God who is bigger than the Enemy, and He has laid a path for all of us if we choose to open the correct gate. On this night, we had chosen the right gate, and along the path Tamika and I were walking, God had placed a nurse full of the Holy Spirit. Before we checked out, she gave us the best gift anyone could have given us that night. Tamika and I were not seeing eye to eye, and our voices had been loud enough for everyone outside our room to hear our argument. I don't know if the nurse had been following our story on Facebook or if she could just see our hearts, but she knew we were being overtaken by the Enemy. She reached out to close the door Tamika and I were walking towards while saying, "I don't always do this; well, sometimes I do when I sense that it's needed. I get the feeling that God has placed you two with me tonight for a reason. Before you leave, I would like for us three to join hands; I need to pray for you."

Her obedience brought tears to my eyes as God used her to bring perspective into our situation. She was able to pray away the Enemy and spoke new life into our marriage and our situation. We hugged her and thanked her for her prayer and walked to the exit door where Tamika and the nurse waited for me to get the car.

When we pulled into our driveway, I told Tamika that I was sorry and explained how hard it had been on me. I told her how much I loved her and how difficult the day had been watching her in pain. "I knew if you had more medicine it might send you over the edge, but I also knew that taking you to the hospital might infect you with something you can't get rid of. Either way, I seemed to lose. Tamika, I did what I felt was best, and I'm sorry that you had to go through this; however, I'm really happy that you are okay. Why don't we just go inside, get some sleep and pray this never happens again."

As we walked into the house, I couldn't help but think about just how close I came to losing my wife that night. I knew that cancer could kill, but how it killed, I wasn't really certain. I thought about the likelihood of Levaquin causing the reaction she had been having for the past five days and how I had tried so hard to make sure everything was done in a way to keep her alive. But even though I followed all the directions of the doctors, she still wound up at the ER fighting for her life. What I realized that night was that neither her doctors nor I could protect her as well as the one who created her, and that is one reason of many as to why we must all put our faith in Him.

After four hours of sleep, we woke up to a Levaquin-free day. Tamika was pain free and thankful to be alive. We talked about the events of the week and contemplated what the next sixteen weeks would have been like had the doctor in the ER not recommended taking the Prilosec at night. We then discussed the timing of the events and how grateful we were that God had paved the way that night.

The week following Levaquin validated what we had hoped was the origin of her pain. Without Levaquin in her system, she was pain free. However, this could have been due to her body recovering from the effects of chemo. There was only one way to find out and that was to go through the next treatment round.

Round Two

♫

Tamika's regimen was, DA-EPOCH-R, included Etoposide, Vincristine, Cyclophosphamide, Doxorubicin, the steroid Prednisolone, and Rituximab, the 'DA' stands for 'dose-adjusted' as the dosage of drugs can be adjusted depending on how your body responds to the treatment. Even though Tamika had the worst week of her life after the first round of chemo, her blood counts stayed normal, which meant the dose should increase during round two.

Tamika is a strong woman who has defeated death twice in her life. The first time was at the age of four when her sister accidentally ran over her twice while backing out of the driveway, and the other was at the age of seventeen when Tamika pulled out in front of a dually truck. The impact on the passenger side caused the front and center pillar to cave in onto her head. The metal sliced her head open folding her scalp over exposing her skull. She was in the hospital for weeks while her badly bruised lungs were on the verge of collapsing. As her family prayed over her, she began to defeat death for the second time. With the history Tamika had endured, I knew if anyone could beat cancer … it was her.

When we entered the hospital, Tamika sported a new look. During the second week, after the first round of chemo, Tamika's hair had started to fall out. To avoid enduring the trauma, she boldly took action against one of the worst parts of chemo for a girl and decided to shave her hair. Prior to chemo, I was worried the hair loss would be too much for Tamika to bear. But Tamika was strong and did not shed a tear as she and a friend took clippers to the remaining amount of her gorgeous, long blonde hair.

Have your ever lived in a moment that you knew was causing you to fall deeper in love with someone? The bravery Tamika displayed while her head was being shaved was one of the moments my love grew for her. I was proud of her for the courage she displayed. As a third grade teacher, Tamika has many young girls who admire her. I would tell Tamika about how proud I was and what an example she was setting for women everywhere. Tamika is a very beautiful lady, and the new look she carried highlighted the features of her face. The way she proudly carried herself without any hair made her more beautiful than ever before.

You see, outward appearance can only get you so far. I think we all know at least one person who has movie star appearance until they open up their mouth and begin to show their heart. At that moment they begin their appearance begins to transform into something ugly. On the contrary, you have probably met a person who most considered to have an ugly appearance until they took time to get to know them. When you can see someone's heart, only then should you make judgment upon their beauty. Luckily for me, I married the best of both. Tamika is radiant on the inside and outside. Even with no hair, there was still a beautiful look about her. Everyone would comment on how great she looked without hair. One night in college, Tamika and I were on a date. Actually, I believe it was an Aerosmith concert in Birmingham. Anyway, after the show was over, a young man stopped me and wanted to shake my hand. He just wanted to let me know that I was one lucky man. He complimented Tamika on her beauty and I replied, "You should know her heart, then you would truly know how beautiful she is."

Let your inner beauty reveal itself.
It takes you to the beauty God meant for you to display.

I remember when one young boy, who couldn't have been more than five years old, saw Tamika and told his mommy to look because she didn't have any hair. I was ahead of Tamika at the time but heard the little boy and turned to see Tamika's reaction. She simply gave him a wink and a smile as she walked passed him. I later asked her if what he said bothered her. She replied that it did not. She expected it and knew that children say innocent things that tend to offend some adults. "I just choose to not be offended. Besides, he's an innocent little boy who just sees life as it is and speaks what he sees."

—————◆—————

Tamika and I had discussed a way to avoid the seven hour wait in the lobby for a room. We decided to arrive early and register with admissions prior to her appointments. Our hope was that a room would be ready by the time we completed her last appointment at 11:00 a.m. Her first appointment was to have her blood drawn for labs, followed by the placement of her PICC line and the visit with her oncologist wrapped up the schedule for the day. If you remember, the PICC line was one of the worst parts of the first round; however, this time Tamika said it went in smoothly and was not nearly as painful as the last.

Shortly after lunch, administration called us to let us know that transportation was on the way down to the lobby to take us to our room. Between the successful plan we'd created and the PICC line placement, round two was off to a much better start. "I wonder if we are going to be on the tenth floor this time?" Tamika asked as we walked to the lobby.

All the buzz about how nice the tenth floor had piqued Tamika's curiosity, resulting in disappointment when she learned that we would once again be on the eleventh floor. However, just like round one, the friendly nurses brought smiles to her face as they raved about Tamika's new look. I remember one particular nurse stopping in to give Tamika a double take and said, "I have to say, you are the most beautiful bald lady I have ever seen." The nurse was right; she was beautiful. I don't know if it was the missing hair or just the way Tamika's inner beauty was showing through, but the new look offered something that seemed to grab everyone's attention.

When Tamika's nurse completed hooking her up to the chemo, the infusions began, and days one, two and three kicked off the week as normal. She would be awake and happy all of day one and most of day two until she grew tired and slept most of the afternoon hours. Day three would begin the first day of nausea, which called for the medicine that would help her rest. This is when my posting on Facebook would normally take place.

Humbled by the demand for a book, I decided to give it a try. I would sit for hours typing away as thoughts of our past came to mind. As I typed away, Tamika rested peacefully while the chemo continued to flow through her veins. The more chemo pumped into her body, the more nauseated she became. By day four and five, Tamika was kept heavily medicated and asleep. All of the quiet time spent alone in the room would have become lonesome had it not been for the new goal of publishing a book. I would write all day while taking brief moments to look up and stare at the lady that I loved so much lying in the bed. I longed to take her place wishing it was me lying there, but it wasn't. God did not place cancer into her body, but He was definitely using it for His glory. I would often walk over to her bed to look at the once healthy young lady who was so full of life and thank Jesus for her while praying for Him to heal her.

The poison that ran through her veins was tearing her body down slowly. Her complexion would turn from a normal light tan to a paler tan during the week of chemo. Her body became weaker as the days moved from Monday to Saturday. By Thursday, the nausea feeling kept her medicated to the point where she slept twenty-two out of twenty-four hours per day. I could see the toll it was beginning to take on her body and wondered how bad it would get. I am a person who likes to be in control, and normally I have a solution for everything. However, I knew that I must continue to give this to Jesus as He is the only one that has a solution for cancer. All I could do was pray that it would be in His will to heal her body.

I was confident that Jesus was with us. If you remember back to the week of Levaquin, a CT scan was performed on Tamika during one of her trips to the ER. It was two weeks after the scan we learned that the results from the scan showed a spot on her kidney that created a lot of concern. I wanted to contact her oncologist immediately; however, her next trip to Vanderbilt was only three days away, so we decided to not panic and trust that it would turn out to be a scar from one of the twelve kidney stones Tamika had passed through the years.

Round Three

⁂

During the first round of chemo, Tamika and I celebrated the fourth of July together in a tiny hospital room on the eleventh floor. I ordered in the only meal Tamika craved throughout the eighteen weeks of treatments, grilled Salmon from Logan's, had a nurse bring in an extra bed sheet to be used as a table cloth and had a romantic dinner date by the window. We hoped to see the nation's second largest firework show outside our window. But the tall building blocking our view allowed us to only see the outer remnants of the bursting bombs in the air. The booms of exploding fireworks echoed through our room leaving us in wonder of how great of a show it must have been.

The third round of chemo interrupted another major event in our life. On August 14, 2014, we celebrated our fifteenth anniversary in the hospital. However, we felt as if it were a little more special as we finally had a room on the tenth floor. The view out of the window was not at all romantic as it overlooked one of the many hospital lobbies, but Tamika and I were set on making the best of what we had to work with when the day came.

The tenth floor room was a lot nicer than the eleventh floor, but I missed the personalities that came with the eleventh floor. Rules were enforced with authority on the tenth floor, and the bubbly relaxed environment was replaced with a business approach. However, we were there for the quality of care, not to be entertained. As the nurses completed the normal first day routine of connecting the lines to Tamika, I prepared my chair/bed for the week. Like a child on Christmas Eve, the morning could not come fast enough for me. I knew the sooner we could get to sleep, the sooner we would learn what the spot on her kidney meant.

If you have ever slept in one of the hospital fold out chairs, you know how difficult it is to get a good night's sleep. This night was no different and was only intensified by my nerves. I tried praying, hoping the burden of anxiety would be taken from me, but my faith was weak that night, and I couldn't help but ponder over the "what ifs" all night long.

Around 7:00 a.m. the doctor walked in to go over the details of the week. The spot was never mentioned during his visit, which gave me the impression the spot was not anything to worry about any longer. But I am a black and white person who doesn't like any gray. I want to know the facts and despise assumptions. Not being able to take another day of not knowing, I asked about the spot before he left the room. He turned around and walked back to her bed and told us they already knew about the spot as it was there on the original scan and was nothing to worry about. "It's just scar tissue, probably from one of your stones," he said as he left the room.

The first night was complete, and we had two more prior to our anniversary date. I worried that Tamika might not feel up to dinner since it would be the end of the third day, which usually left her feeling nauseas. We decided to have dinner one night early, so once again, I ordered in the salmon from Logan's and together we celebrated our milestone in the hospital bed, watching a movie and reflecting on our life together. After the many years of choosing the wrong gates, it felt peaceful knowing that we were now choosing the gates that led to the path our Lord had prepared for us.

Hidden Blessings

ℐℐ

Before I entered Kindergarten, we lived on a small farm. I think back to the life we had on the farm often. Even though I was young, I can remember the house very well. It was a large house that sat about three hundred yards off the road with steps that were perfect for sliding down on your bottom. My sister and I used to race down the steps to see who could slide down them the fastest. Driving up the long driveway, you would see the barn that was halfway from the road to the house. In front of the barn sat two outhouses. Why they were there, I had no idea. However, they made a great spot to hide when playing hide and seek. I don't know if my sister was too scared to check in them or if she just never thought that I would be bold enough to hide in an outhouse. When I first started hiding inside them, I thought for sure I would be caught. After all, they sat out in the middle of the field and were very obvious, but no one ever found me.

Blessings are a lot like that hiding spot. They tend to sit right in front of us yet are somehow overlooked. Similar to hide and seek, you have to be open-minded and think outside of the box to begin seeing the blessings that are hidden. I know when Tamika was first diagnosed with cancer, all my mind wanted to do was think about the negative what if's. I knew that I needed to change my perspective in order to see God's work, so I decided to stop focusing on the "what if" and started focusing on finding the blessings.

The month I lost my job, two reps from my life insurance company stopped by my house to try and upsell me. Since I wasn't home, they left a card on the door asking to give them a call, which I ignored since I had just lost my job. A couple of weeks later, they stopped by again, and once again, I wasn't home. This time I took their card and kept it in my wallet. The intention I had was to contact them the first week of June; if I had a job, I would listen to them, otherwise I was canceling my cancer policy to improve the budget. The reps were persistent and came back in mid-May and caught me at home. Seeing no way out, I decided to be upfront and honest with them. After listening to their spiel about how I could switch over to a lifetime cancer policy for only two dollars more a month, I informed them about my situation and how I was not raising any bills. In fact, if I wasn't employed by June, I was planning on cancelling. Once again, they gave it one more try and told me that by switching over to lifetime, if someone in my family was diagnosed with cancer, the current policy would only cover them once. If they ever developed cancer again, there would not be any benefits. "By switching over to the lifetime, there will always be benefits no matter how many times they battle cancer. It's only two dollars more a month, sir; please consider doing this. You never know what might happen."

I told them, "no one in my family had cancer and we didn't plan on getting it. I don't need any more debt; I need a job." To that the reps left and I went back to searching online for job opportunities. Little did I know what a blessing I was about to miss out on.

If you remember, when Tamika was having her biopsy performed, I was waiting in the room, praying for her. During that time, God reminded me about the cancer policy. I could tell it was urgent, so I took time out of praying to place a call to the reps. Neither answered the call, so I left a message for them to call back. It was five hours after the call before I heard from either one of them, and when I did, I was told that as long as she does not have a diagnosis, then it's not too late to sign the papers. The conversation took place the morning Tamika was at home and felt so bad that my cousin had to drive us back to the hospital. The reps had to be somewhere within the hour and only had a few minutes to wait on us. When we pulled up, they were there with pen and papers in hand. Tamika had been throwing up all morning, and I'm sure she was not too fond of me pushing her to the side for a minute while I signed the papers, but she was in no shape to try to understand the importance of what I was doing. After signing the papers, I thanked them for waiting on us and briefly told them what a miracle it was that I did not cancel earlier in the month. Between the cancer policy and the money raised for my family, we were able to sustain our bills for six months.

God has been and will always be good to us. I remember the time when I could not see the blessings He provided, and now that I am walking with Christ, I see them daily. Most of the time, the blessings do not appear in the form of money, but during Tamika's treatments, money is what we needed and God always provided. The best example I can think of is when our car was broken down and we were scraping the bottom of our account to pay the $761.00 repair bill. Tamika had to be at her oncologist the next day for labs, and I wasn't sure how we were going to pay for the gas since we just emptied the account. But when we got home and checked the mail, I found a check for $765.00. I sat down and looked at the check with a heart full of faith and tears in my eyes. I really could not believe what I was looking at. I knew that God had lined up a miracle on that day. His timing is perfect, and I was convinced that He really had paved the way for our family.

Tamika completed round four, five and six without any major issues. A PET scan was performed before her fifth and after her sixth rounds of chemo. Both resulted in negative results and no sign of the tumor at all. The chemo had dissolved it, and we had stomped on the Enemy's head. Following her last scan, I started my new job with the company that interviewed me two days prior to us discovering the tumor in June 2014.

Finding Hope

CID

After losing my job and learning about Tamika's cancer diagnosis, I was trying to find some hope. I knew that hope could be found in Christ, which led me to setting up the Facebook page to ask everyone I knew to pray for her. Prayer changes things; Jesus tells us this in Matthew 18:19-20. So if this is true, why don't we all pray as if it is? Why don't we all trust that God will pull us through everything? I know that one of my reasons for not praying like this was due to having a control issue prior to Tamika's cancer. That may be true for you too. If so, don't let a tragedy or a doctor's report be the reason you decide to pray hard. Pray hard daily, search out for God and listen for Him to direct you to the gate He has for you.

My dad saw the cup as half empty and lost hope on finding a better way. Drowning himself in alcohol was the way he dealt with his wound that never healed. The wound that was opened up at such a young age plagued him throughout his entire life. Don't let what happened to him happen to you. If you have a wound that needs healing, speak life into it by focusing on the good that has come from it. If you cannot find the good, search harder. It is there. God is everywhere and loves to take horrible situations and turn them around for His glory. Look around you and find the hidden blessings that have been overlooked so many times. Trust me; they are there. They were placed there by God, and He has been waiting to show you the blessings. And when you do find them, speak them by sharing your testimony. Doing so will set you free of what currently binds you. There is healing in sharing your testimony. Open up your heart and forgive the ones that have you bound with unforgiveness. Begin to walk daily with Christ and follow Him forever by developing a relationship with Him. Without Jesus, we are all lost in an immoral world. If God is love, without Him there would be no good left in this world.

Contrary to what mainstream media, social media and hearsay leads us to believe, THERE IS GOOD in this world. Sometimes, we just have to dig deep to find it. I created the Pray for Tamika Powell Facebook page selfishly. I wanted my wife to live, and I believed the more people that prayed for her, the more likely God would answer the prayers. The prayers were answered in so many ways and as time passed by, we began receiving feedback from random people. Some were friends while others we had never met. We would listen to them as they shared to us how being able to walk along side of us during our journey was such a blessing. They would tell us how inspiring it was and how it had changed their perspective and strengthened their faith. Prior to June, 2014, I participated in social media as little as I could as I believed in was nothing except a way to waste away life. However, I learned if used properly, social media could be used in great ways. For us, it provided hope, truth about life, love, hard times, sorrow and sadness. But most importantly, it let people know that they were not alone in the battles we all face.

I chose to write this book to share my life with others. I want to expose my flaws to let people know that I have messed up too. I was once an addict who eventually went bankrupt, nearly lost his family, cursed God and emotionally abused his spouse. But somehow, I survived it all and found Christ along the way. He used me just like He had used many others who battled worse problems than I battled. Just like the way He can use you if you let Him.

Honestly, I'm no one special, just a simple man who decided to write a book to share my struggles in life. In reality, my struggles really can't compare to others who go through much worse. You may have been thinking while reading my book about how much more difficult your life has been than mine and rightfully so. But remember that we all have one thing in common and that is finding hope. When the world has beaten you down and you are feeling like giving up, don't. There is another gate that offers a new path, and the key to that gate is held by Jesus. All you have to do is seek Him and ask Him to help you find His path. But be aware, the Enemy is sneaky and will be waiting for you to slip up. And when you do, don't give in, instead push forward; Jesus is with you; He will never leave you. But you must call out to Him and seek Him daily. Find a church home, but make sure it's one that you enjoy and get involved! Most importantly, always remember to Pray Hard and Speak Life.

Acknowledgements

I am so blessed to have the support from such wonderful friends and family members along with the best local and online community who all came together to make sure this was a success. All of you have believed in me from the very beginning and I am forever grateful.

To Tamika, you have been a shining light in my darkest hour. I will always love you and I look forward to our front porch swing.

To my mom, I am the man I am today because of you and dad. Thank you for all the life lessons as well as enduring all the pain I created when I ignored them. I love you and could not have a more loving mom.

To Troy, thank you for sharpening me. You have endured many of my agonizing questions and debates. Your family is such a blessing to mine and we love you all so much.

To Kelly, thank you for allowing me to interrupt your day with questions that pertain to my writings.

To Jennifer Cupp, thank you for being the answer to a prayer which was the turning point to the decision to publish this book.

To Pastor Jerry, thank you for following God's lead in your life. Future generations of my family have been changed by the message God gave you on generational curses. I am forever grateful for your obedience to speak the truth to the congregation at Daystar Church.

To Julie Scroggins, thank you for reading drafts of my book over and over to help me fine tune the words I wanted to share.

To Karen Morris and Melanie Maddox, thank you for taking time to help shape this book into what it is today.

To Kori Brown Wiginton, thank you for being the sweet, lovable person you are but most importantly, thank you for not renting the movie so many years ago. Who knows where I would be today if you had not told me no.

To the Super Six, thank you for reading the original draft and providing the feedback needed to bring this book to life.

To all 1,163 members of the Pray for Tamika Facebook page, thank you for praying hard and speaking life throughout Tamika's battle with cancer as well as encouraging me to write this book.

To Shana, thank you for the wonderful necklace you made for Tamika while she was battling cancer. Bet you never thought it would be on the cover of a book.

To everyone who supported my Kickstarter campaign, thank you so much for believing in me!!

God bless you all for being who you are.

With Love,
Clifton J. Powell

About the Author

Clifton J Powell was born in 1976 in Cullman, AL where he graduated from Cullman High School in 1995. Powell left Cullman for the University of Alabama where he earned a Bachelor of Science degree in Education. There he found his wife, Tamika and together they have four children; Brannon, Mandolyn, Lillyann, Melody and their Maltese named Trooper. After graduating college Clifton spent fifteen years gaining knowledge about people in the career of sales. In 2014, Clifton found a love for writing while sharing stories about how their marriage came to be on his wife's Facebook prayer page. The writings became very popular and a demand for a book led to him writing Pray Hard & Speak Life.

Made in the USA
Lexington, KY
14 January 2018